A New Vision for
DATING

FINDING GOD'S PLAN FOR A NEW RELATIONSHIP

STACY HORD

BRIDGE
LOGOS
FOUNDATION

Alachua, Florida 32615

Bridge-Logos
Alachua, FL 32615 USA

A New Vision for Dating
by Stacy Hord

Edited by Mary Ruth Murray

Library of Congress Catalog Card Number: 2009937052
International Standard Book Number 978-0-88270-9253

G163.316.N.m909.35230

Dedication

My dearest Kim, because of you I understand God's faithfulness. I have never known anyone more Christ-like than you are. Your friendship has made me who I am. Thank you.

Sydney, my sister, you've always been there for me. I love you!

Dallas, Dalton, and Dylan; I've never laughed harder and loved deeper than I have with you. Everything I do, I do for you.

To my friend and Lord, Jesus Christ, the Light of my life. Thank you for bringing me into the wonderful plan of yours.

Contents

Introduction   vii

NEW BEGINNINGS

1   The Night That Changed Everything   1

2   The Judge, the Attorney, and the Prosecutor   7

3   Leah's Honeymoon   15

4   Get Out the Artillery   21

PUT YOUR PAST TO REST AND MOVE ON

5   The Ball and Chain   29

6   Hummingbirds   37

7   Fatherless Memories   43

8   No Limits, No Boundaries   51

A NEW VISION FOR A NEW KIND OF RELATIONSHIP

9   What's a Dysfunctional Relationship?   59

10   Attraction Isn't the Only Thing   65

11   Taking Responsibility for Your Relationship   73

12   The Sleeping Giant   79

PRACTICING TO BE A GOOD MATE

13   For Richer or Poorer   91

14   Slicing and Dicing   97

15 Loneliness—Let It Serve a Purpose in Your Life 103

16 Those Crazy Button Pushers! 111

In Those Times of Doubt

17 When God Comes on the Scene 119

18 How Will I Ever Meet Someone? 125

19 You Can, You Must, and You Will! 133

20 Why Am I Waiting on God Anyway? 139

21 Our Precious Desert Experience 145

What's Ahead for You?

22 Restoration Is for *You!* 153

23 The Mercy of God 159

24 Can You and I Really Trust God? 165

Three Things That Will Change Your Life

25 When You Need Answers 173

26 If I Could Go Back and Do It All Again . . . 179

27 Creating Your Legacy 187

Conclusion 195

Lonely and Hurting Singles, Please Enter This Door

We were just beginning a new session of a divorce recovery workshop and our small support group of nine—three men and six women—pulled our chairs into a circle formation to discuss the video we had just watched. I had been a facilitator and teacher for the program for several years and I still found that the first night of the workshop was the hardest for the participants.

Across the large room were hurting people seated at eight tables just like ours, anxious to get on the road to healing. Within minutes the sounds of many voices speaking, whispering, and crying filled the air as people began to share their sorrows. As I scanned the room and saw the faces of those that had come for help, my heart ached. I am well acquainted with the long journey on which these seekers were about to embark, the journey of healing and trying to figure out what to do next with their lives. It definitely does not happen overnight and it takes an open mind and plenty of commitment. I knew that by the end of the ten-week workshop, many would drop out, unable or unwilling to finish the course. Those that finished, on the other hand, would step out into their new single life, armed and encouraged.

Six years earlier, I had enrolled in the same program as an eager participant, anxious to have my divorce behind me and ready to get on with my new life. At the time, I was already dating, although I was only legally separated. It just seemed like the natural progression of things. Once you are out of a bad relationship, you get right back on the horse and find a new one. I even remember thinking that I might meet someone in my divorce recovery group. I gave the workshop 100 percent of my effort and found that the sessions did me a world of good. I was on the road to healing and was asked to become a facilitator and later Co-Director for the program.

When a new session begins, as a facilitator I customarily ask each person in the group to introduce themselves and give a short summary of their divorce story. I always make sure there are plenty of tissue boxes on hand, for the stories are truly heartbreaking. This night was no different.

We started with one of the women. Married for sixteen years to her college sweetheart, there seemed to be no real indication of trouble except for the occasional grumpiness that husbands can exhibit. But one day her life was shattered when he confessed to her that he had never really loved her and wanted to move out. I already knew what was coming next as she cried, "He moved in with my best friend two weeks later." She continued, "It's especially hard to send my kids over to their house. Those are the worst weekends. I usually end up crying most of the weekend from the loneliness. My friends want to set me up with a guy they know and I'm thinking about going. I'm just so lonely."

As we continued around the circle, the stories were different, but the effects of the divorces were the same: empty houses, empty lives, failure, and loneliness. We finally came to the last person, a woman. This had been her third marriage and it lasted only two years. She gave a short version of how her husband was mentally abusive to the point where she could no longer stay with him. A tear slipped down her cheek as she expressed her hopes. "I just know the right person is out there—the one that will treat me like a queen. I won't stop looking because I believe he really exists."

I hid my outward reaction while I sighed inwardly. I have heard it over and over again in our workshop: the rebound phenomenon. This woman had already set her sights on getting back on the trail to finding a new love before being healed from the last one, or the one before that. Her thoughts had already moved ahead and she was dreaming of "the one." Her current mental state was forcing her more into fantasy than reality and she wanted a knight in shining armor to come and make it all better.

It's not that I haven't had that same thought at least a hundred times. When a relationship fails, our hearts are screaming for some kind of retribution. There is a hole and a loss and we want that hole filled and that loss made right. We want the whole world, and especially our exes, to see that we are still desirable, and the quicker the better. We need to show we can bounce back. Who cares that we are carrying baggage from all the way back to our childhood? Who cares that we will be taking our anger and bitterness into a new relationship? A new person is the answer. All of our old habits will change, because, of course, that new person will only bring out the good in us. Life will be grand with that new person. Hollywood has it right. Keep floating in and out of exciting, romantic relationships. As soon as one goes bad, line up another one. Just stay on the merry-go-round and keep going round, and round, and round.

Her statement moved me to say something that I always say to my groups, but this time I tried to sound as straightforward and sincere as I could. Lives were at stake here. I looked at each one and began slowly. "I'm going to ask you to do something that may be a little hard for you, but I want you to trust me on this. I'm asking you not to date, or even think about dating while you are taking this course. It will only be two months, and after that, you can do whatever you want. I know this doesn't make sense now, but the *last* thing you need at this time is a date. If you will give God this time to show you some new things, and if you will open your heart to challenge traditional thinking, I think you'll be surprised at how much healing and change can occur in your lives. You must learn to be a successful single person before you can be in a successful marriage, so please consider this request."

The woman who had been married three times was the most affected by this statement. Obviously, this put a screeching halt on her plans to find a new man by the weekend. She showed her frustration as she countered my request. "What's wrong with my dating? I'm lonely and I need someone. You don't know how lonely I get living in a house by myself!" I assured her that I have also dealt with extreme loneliness, but I have also dealt with the consequences of dating when it was too soon and I wasn't ready.

I then told my table of listeners my own story.

When my husband and I agreed to separate and he moved out of the house, the marriage was already over in our minds. There was no talk of counseling or reconciliation and neither of us was exactly seeking the Lord for wisdom in the matter. Then, to hammer another nail in the coffin, we both began dating others before the divorce was even final. I had a scrapbook of memories I could retrieve and replay in my mind at any time to justify my need for hitting the dating scene so early. I reasoned that he was mean and abusive and he had robbed me of years of happiness.

Well, I would fix that! I would just go find my prince. He would be wildly handsome and mysterious, wise beyond his years, generous, and much more romantic than the grouch I had just wasted years on. So I formed my girlfriend posse and we were out every weekend hitting the hot spots, searching for my prince.

At first, it was all good and I landed dates immediately. I was flying high, being wined, and dined. Then I gradually found myself in despair because none of those men was working out. My despair turned to desperation and as I progressed in my disillusionment, I began sinking lower and lower in a pit of confusion and fruitless ventures. I used men and I was used. The world is a rough place and it can chew you up and spit you out. I found that out the hard way.

Oh, I was so stupid! There is just no other way to put it. The things I did the following year in search of my prince still make me cringe. And I realize now that I was actually prolonging my healing instead of helping myself. Dr. Henry Cloud says in his book, Changes That Heal, "Hurt always interferes with clear thinking." I had been hurt and I was not thinking clearly. The fog I was in was sending me into a tailspin of wrong relationships and further hurt. I needed a miracle to get off the crazy ride I was on.

Thank God that miracle came. I cried out to God and He put me on a new path. But in order to be totally attentive and focused on that path, I needed to take a short break from dating. When I allowed God that special time, a literal miracle of healing changed me to the very core of my soul.

As I sat at the table with my newly divorced little lambs, my heart ached. I knew, I was looking into the faces of some that were about to make the same mistakes. I knew how alone they felt and I knew that some of them were already in new relationships and exhibiting some of the same behavior patterns as in their previous relationships. If they were not already with another person, they were scouting for one. They were hitting the bars, churches, singles events, and the Internet hoping to find "the one." They had tunnel vision. The teaching in this class was all fine and good to relieve some hurt, but they needed their relationship *fix*.

Half of this group had been married before and most would likely marry again—some of them very soon. I see it happen all the time and those second marriages do not always turn out for the best. We have all seen the statistics on second marriages. Seventy-five percent of them are doomed to fail. But when you're not thinking clearly in the first place, it is easy to believe that statistics are for *other* people.

As it turned out, the woman who was on her third divorce never came back to the sessions. Another woman took the route I had taken earlier—looking for love in all the wrong places—and she ended up being tragically raped after a night of too many cocktails. Five sessions into the course, one of the remaining women went on a blind date and told us about it in class. She was frustrated that it was not what she had hoped for, and was feeling like there were just no *good guys* left in this world. Her loneliness and rejection were reaffirmed, and she was worse off than if she had never gone on the date.

Only one man took me up on my challenge. He told me that he was inspired that an attractive woman would choose not to date, for a period of time, to allow God to renew her from the inside. He knew that if I could do it, he could do it, and he would trust God to do some great things in his life during that time. He stuck to his word for the duration of the sessions and kept in contact with me for several months. He was dealing with his loneliness in positive ways by restoring his relationship with his kids and going deeper in his walk with God. I was thrilled when he unexpectedly called me to tell me that he had experienced an overwhelming sense of joy all day. He could not explain it; he just felt happy and had to tell someone. He gave all the credit to God and it was obvious that he was experiencing some real spiritual growth in his life. Oh, he still had his lonely moments, but he was dealing with them with strength from on high. This was remarkable for a man who wanted to die just a few short months earlier.

There are many reasons why men and women date and marry too soon after a failed relationship. However, let me give a few reasons why you should consider taking a short time out before returning to the dating scene.

1. Some of the reasoning is as elementary as the fact that *you need to be fixed.* When my car has accumulated a lot of miles, I take time out for an oil change and tire rotation. When a runner has run so many marathons that his knees are failing, it is time to give the knees a rest and let the doctor tend to them. You get the point. When your heart has been cheated and hurt, or it's in a confused state, it's time to take a short break and tend to it. Better yet, it is time to let the Great Physician tend to it. He will nurse it, soothe it, and make it stronger. When you are better, He will release you to go share your newly healed heart with another, and with His blessing.

2. Another reason for taking a time out is the all too real danger and consequence of landing in another unhealthy relationship.

It's true—like attracts like. If you are emotionally unhealthy, your unhealthy energy will be a magnet for another unhealthy person of the opposite sex. I hear it all the time: "I always attract the crazy ones." There is a good reason for that. Sometimes you have been in your unhealthy state for so long, it has become comfortable, and it is home. When unhealthy relationships are all you have known, it feels right. The presence of a healthy person can actually feel wrong and uncomfortable because it's foreign and strange. That's a pit you definitely want to get out of before it claims all the opportunities for real love in your life. God can bring to light all the issues that are blocking your ability to have relationships with healthy people.

I will admit, it actually felt a little strange when I started conversing with healthy people in healthy communication. I had always loved the *bad boys*, while the *nice guys* were too straight and churchy for me. Somehow, the drama that accompanied those bad relationships gave me a distorted, but powerful, high. Sometimes during my healing, I even felt a longing to go back to those crazy relationships. During the renewal process, our flesh still wrestles with us, desiring to go back to the only thing we know and are comfortable with. However, through the power of Christ, my discernment began to grow and when God brought me to a strong realization that these *bad boys* were really just unhealthy, spiritually immature (or vacant) people, I saw them in a new light. I could have compassion and concern for them, but I kept my distance. No more unhealthy relationships for me, and I now find the *nice guys* very appealing and attractive.

3. The third reason to take a time out is to make sure you are mentally ready to detect a counterfeit—a person that initially charms your socks off, but eventually turns out to be a fake and regrettably, a horrible mistake.

A friend of mine is a reporter and anchorperson for a local news affiliate. She educated me about child abuse one day and told me that around 80 percent of child molestations and rapes stem from the mother's relationships with boyfriends and new husbands. Some of those mothers have been in my workshops. I have personally met many good women who unknowingly brought a molester into their homes who preyed on their children. They didn't mean to, it's just that they were lonely and he was so charming and understanding. Proverbs 27:7 (NIV) explains it this way: *"He who is full loathes honey, but to the hungry even what is bitter tastes sweet.*" If your heart is starving, and your mind is not clear, you will take almost anyone into your life, *and* the lives of your loved ones.

To bring a new stepfather or live-in boyfriend into the home of adolescent girls can be quite traumatizing in its own right. Fathers and daughters have a natural, wholesome relationship. The daughter never has to second-guess her father's presence or attention to her. However, when an unrelated man moves into the home, the young girl's safety mechanisms are heightened. Her comfort level will change and some experts even suggest that introducing the pheromones of a new man into the home can actually stimulate physical changes in a pre-adolescent girl, sending her into puberty sooner than other girls who live with their natural father.

While boys may not suffer from the same effects, they find sharing their mom with a new man to be extremely challenging and frustrating. They may even feel a sense of loss as mom's attention is diverted to another male. Young girls can experience the same loss when Dad brings a new woman into their life. Don't get me wrong; I am not saying that remarriage is bad, just do it in God's time and with wisdom, so that it brings enrichment to your life, not complications and trouble.

A year after our divorce, I came face to face with the truth of these statistics and facts and found myself having to make a decision. I had spent the previous year dating and living it up (which got me exactly nowhere). My ex-husband was also distracted with a new girlfriend and I could see the toll it was taking on the children. The oldest child commented that he felt like he was on the back burner while the new girlfriend was getting all of his dad's time. I was heartbroken. This just was not working. I was spinning my wheels in senseless relationships, and my kids were the burnt rubber left on the road.

I cried out to God asking Him if it was too late for things to change. His answer was, "It is never too late." After several weeks of prayer, I had an ever-increasing feeling that I needed to take a time out from dating, even for just a short while. God wanted to show me a new vision for my life and He needed my undivided attention. Not only that, the children needed my undivided attention. I had no more arguments left. I had made a lot of mistakes and it was clear that my way just was not cutting it. I agreed with God that I would do it His way.

I made the decision to take a short time out from dating and a new adventure started almost immediately. God's supernatural power began helping me in many ways. A couple of weeks into my new commitment, I received a call from a man that I had dated several months earlier who had recently moved back to town. He was one of those men that could still make me weak with longing, as he was very attractive and extremely charismatic. Never mind that he was not a Christian; none of the guys I had dated during that time were, even though I knew better.

As I reached for my phone, the caller ID was unmistakable, but instead of my heart leaping for joy, I was mildly annoyed. In his charming voice, he began telling me how much he had missed me and wanted to see me. I mentally yawned. I politely told him that I wasn't interested in seeing anyone, hoped that he was doing well, and thanked him for calling. His reply was worth a hundred dollars: "You're saying you don't want to see me?"

I honestly did not want to see him. Something had changed in me. I was home alone and I was okay with it. I just wanted to curl up in bed and watch a good movie. I spoke to him for no longer than a minute—just enough time to convince him that I had no more interest in him. After I hung up the phone, I sat down to ponder what had just happened. I had just turned down a date with someone that only months earlier had a powerful hold on me. I exclaimed out loud, "This *has* to be God!" It felt good.

A few days later, I nonchalantly mentioned to my sons that I had no more interest in dating and would be focusing all my time on them and their activities. I'm not sure they bought it at first, but within a few weeks it was becoming apparent to them that they were the only men in my life. If someone posed the question of my dating status, I made sure that my kids were within earshot to hear me say that I was just enjoying the company of my sons too much and didn't want to miss a second of being with them. It didn't take long for my boys to see that this was for real.

My heart was changing. I wasn't wondering what my friends were out doing on the weekends. I didn't care. And God was good in turning the hearts of my sons toward me and restoring our home life. There were times the boys and I piled on my bed to watch TV together, laughing and teasing each other until our stomachs hurt. I thought in my heart, "There is no date that can compare to this!"

I have seen my sons' confidence grow since I made the decision to do this God's way. There is a stability and security in their life that Mom's not going anywhere and God is in control. God has miraculously erased their memories of how I was before and imprinted on their hearts a picture of a mother who is totally in love with Jesus.

After a few months without dating, my thinking progressively changed as my mind was being renewed. God revealed areas in my own life that had contributed to the downfall of my relationships—areas that I would have remained blind to if I had not allowed Him the time to teach me. He taught me how to retrain my thinking about life, men, and marriage, and showed me how to distinguish between healthy and unhealthy relationships. Most importantly, He showed me how my connection to Him would dictate whether I would be fruitful in future relationships. *I had to be anchored in His love before I could love another.* God then began to show me His vision for my life. It was greater than I could have ever dreamed and more than I would have ever dared to ask for.

It has been four years now since I made that decision, and although I only meant to hold off dating for just a year, I am truly content and have not returned to the dating scene yet. Now, do I hope to be re-married some day? Absolutely! I'm counting on it. That's part of the new vision.

I know you're thinking that you have no desire to go four years without dating, and I have no intention of trying to persuade you to do that. I am just asking you to consider refraining from the dating scene for a few weeks, about the length of time it will take to read this book. When you spend a short season of time just focused on God and His direction for your life, He can show you things about yourself that you have never seen before and lead you to change behaviors that will keep you from repeating past mistakes. The chapters in this book are designed to take you through steps of recovery while building a vision for your exciting future. Each chapter will address you both as a single person and as a prospective mate in the future. I am hoping that you will reflect long and hard about your life, and where you want to go with it, as you develop a new perspective of God's role in your future decisions.

Faith gets ready and if you are anticipating that God has someone for you, the time to prepare for a successful relationship is *now*. You must transform your thinking and behavioral patterns to those that will work *for* you and not against you. This means opening yourself up to embrace a change of direction in some of the sensitive areas of your life. When Jesus wanted to teach others about the Kingdom of God, He had one prerequisite: you must become like a child again. You must put away all the old things in your life and start anew. You must become vulnerable again, trusting, and thirsty to learn. If you come to Him in this way, new things will be opened up to you.

The real vision and pulse of this book is restoration. The Bible is full of verses that display God's heart for restoration. Not a restoration as we know it—returning something back to its original state—but a restoration that makes you *better* than you were before, and your pains and struggles are forgotten because God's blessing on your life outweighs all of your painful past.

Return, you exiles who now have hope; return to your place of safety. Now I tell you I will repay you twice over with blessing for all you have suffered. (Zechariah 9:12, GNT)

For every mistake you have made in the past, every hurt you have ever had, every bad relationship you have experienced, He wants to restore two-fold to you in blessings and hope. That is *more* than you had before. It is just God's way. When he restores a life, he takes that person higher than they would have even dreamed to go. He is the ultimate giver.

If you have just come out of a divorce, separation, or long relationship and are thinking that the answer to your pain is to go find another relationship, I beg you to reconsider for at least a few weeks. Then after you have read this book, you can date your whole town, if that is your desire. But I'm hoping that after you read my testimony you might have a change of heart.

Just take one day at a time, read a chapter, and ask God what he wants you to do with that chapter. Time will be your friend and God will use it to stretch you, grow you, and change you. Learning patience and perseverance over the next few weeks will be one of the tools that will transform your life. I highly recommend involving your friends and family for support and accountability. Don't be surprised if they are a little intrigued by all this. I always receive admiration and respectful compliments from others when they learn that I am going against the grain of society and not rushing into another relationship.

One other thing: don't be surprised at all if suddenly someone approaches you for a date. The devil is pretty sneaky sometimes and knows how to throw you off track. If you have given this time to God and entered into a commitment with Him, *He* won't be the one sending tempting eye candies into your life. God will protect you, and empower you, if you ask Him. As for me, I am going to pray for you right now because I believe in the power of prayer:

Dear Father,

I pray for the beautiful person that is reading this book at this moment, your child, whom you love so much. You know every thought we have. You know every hurt and question we have had about our lives, and you have all the answers because you see into our future. I ask you to open the eyes and heart of this person to discover the vision you have for his or her life, and shield them from the enemy. Start working restoration in their life right now, today. Fill them with your Spirit, your hope, and your promises. Teach them to persevere while they wait, and in the meantime, reveal yourself to them in ways they have never known you before.

In the name of Jesus, I humbly ask all these things. Amen.

New Beginnings

One day while out taking a walk, I felt an urge to take a different route from my regular path. I soon found myself on a beautiful road with signs that read "Meredith Gardens." I never knew that a scenic garden was so close to my house and within walking distance.

To my delight, I found a large waterfall surrounded by beautiful gardens, creating a small paradise. I wondered, "How in the world did I not know this was here?"

God whispered in my heart, "Because this is the first time you were willing to take a different route."

Leave your regular path and come along with me …

CHAPTER ONE

The Night That Changed Everything

It was 2:30 A.M. and I was driving home alone after a long night of partying. Only I was not in the party mood anymore. I was crying and I was miserable. Mascara and tears cascaded down my face as a fifty-pound weight of depression and shame descended on me. Things had to change. I was so sick of it all—the alcohol, the shallow men, the drama—the whole party lifestyle. I wish I could say my heart was hurting, but it was completely numb and void. It was my spirit that was hurting.

After my husband and I separated, almost a year before the divorce was finalized, I did what so many newly single people do. I partied, I had boyfriends, and I made unwise decisions. The party crowd was more than happy to accept me as one of their own and I had plenty of friends to help me celebrate my new status as a single woman.

When the divorce was final, I pursued my activities with even more intensity and vengeance. Oh, it was fun at first, but somewhere along the line, the fun subtly turned into a meaningless existence without purpose. I hadn't noticed at first, but these lonely car rides home were becoming excruciating. There was no fruit in this kind of life and the emptiness seemed to hit hardest on the drive home. I felt like I was returning home from being nowhere—just a black vortex of shallow conversation, empty relationships, and nothingness. It was as if I had gotten all dressed up to go sit in a dark hole all night and then drove home. My mind was also becoming dark and I was constantly preoccupied with concerns about my love life, which was horribly painful.

Although I was a Christian who had attended church all my life, and had raised my kids in church, I had no recent contact with God. My prayers had dwindled down to occasional pleas for Him not to send me to hell because of the way I was living. I just did not feel like praying anymore. Moreover, I could not shake a sense of guilt and hopelessness that drove me further away from a God that I considered too holy to get close to a sinner like me. The distance took its toll on me, and I had become empty, and dry, without emotion. Plus, I was hiding from God. If I didn't pray, I didn't have to account for my behavior.

But that night I was heartsick, torn, depressed, and without hope. I had hit bottom, and bottom was a long way down in a deep, dark pit. There was only one Person who could reach deep enough into that pit to raise me out and I knew He was the only Person who still loved a blubbering, mascara smeared, messed up girl like me. I had turned away from Him long enough. It was time to turn *toward* Him.

I just needed to say His name. I could not say or even form a whole prayer; I was too dry and raw. But I knew that there was so much power in just saying His name, it would be enough. He would know why I was saying it and He would respond in the same way as if Mother Teresa had said it. I knew in my heart He would hear. Something told me I had a heavenly audience.

I opened my mouth and I softly whispered, "Jesus." I said it again—"Jesus"—all while I was driving on the highway in my car. I started to say it louder, over, and over, "Jesus," all the way home. That is all I said that night, and that is all He needed.

A few days later, I went to church. It was still a challenge for me to be in a place that piqued my conviction to the point I almost couldn't stand it, but I staggered through it. After the service, I walked out to my car to wait for my sons to get out of their teen service. As I sat in my car, I saw the mother of one of the church teens walking across the parking lot, heading directly for me. "Oh, puh-leese!" I thought. "I don't feel like talking to anyone right now. I'm sure she's coming to tell me how much she has missed me lately and her words to me will no doubt be filled with churchy fluff and syrupy, sweet talk. I grudgingly rolled down the window and put on my best fake smile. "Hi, how are you?" I warily chirped.

She stood outside my car, said a few pleasantries, and then softly asked, "Are you okay?"

"I think I am, thanks for asking." I was still hiding out emotionally from everyone.

Undeterred, she continued. She had a mission and needed to tell me something. She began, "The other night, I woke up in the middle of the night, around two or three in the morning, and you were on my mind. I just started praying for you. I didn't know what was going on; I just knew I needed to pray. Is everything okay with you?"

I teared up slightly and responded in low tones as my sons approached the car, "I appreciate your prayers. Please keep praying." That's all I said to her and then she left.

As my sons and I headed home, I began to make the connection. A few nights earlier, on that lonely drive home from partying, I had felt the need to cry out to God. All I'd said was the name "Jesus." I could not form a complete prayer, so He called on someone else to finish that prayer for me. And, as it turned out, she wasn't the only one He had been calling on to pray for me. My best friend of fifteen years had been crying out to God on my behalf and so had several others. The ice was melting in my heart. I was feeling hope again. God really cared. He cared enough to wake someone up in the middle of the night to pray for me. More importantly, I began to realize something even more shocking. He wasn't mad at me, He was feeling compassion for me.

I don't know what happens in Heaven when we say the name "Jesus." Maybe big red lights flash and a huge bell rings so that all of Heaven can hear the "Jesus Hotline" sounding. Maybe the sound of millions of people around the Earth saying "Jesus" forms a beautiful melody and a sweet fragrance that drifts up to the throne and the Father inhales it like sweet incense. Maybe every time the name of Jesus is sounded in Heaven, everyone there drops down to their knees immediately because the power of His name forces them to worship and glorify Him. I don't know. But I *do* know that when we call on His name, something powerful happens; something that we cannot see, but that indisputably happens. He hears it.

He turns His head to the one who is calling out and sees all the way down into their soul. He doesn't waste a second! Before His name is barely off our lips, He acts. He begins appointing angels, sending ministering spirits, and calling faithful prayer warriors to pray on our behalf. Then He does one more thing. He takes His hand and begins to reach down, down, into a long, dark, slimy pit, for that one who sits at the bottom calling out for Him—you and me. His fingers finally touch you and He wraps them tenderly around your whole being. Then He slowly begins to lift, taking care that you're eased up gently as He raises you all the way to the top. He then plants your feet on solid ground and guards you like a hawk because you are His beloved and He is jealous for you.

This is the first and most crucial step in your healing from all your past mistakes: calling out to Jesus and allowing Him to put you in a new place while He watches over you. We can go no further into a new vision for your future until you have a firm understanding that your very life depends on Him. You *must* know that you can call on Him in any situation and He will come to your aid, no questions asked. No pit is too deep or too gross for Him and no sins are too scandalous or perverted for Him. His arm is long enough and His hand is strong enough to reach all of us no matter where we are.

Even more remarkable, He does not require that we clean up our act first. He meets us where we are. No conditions need to be met and no vows need to be made. He already fulfilled all those requirements when He took them upon himself and paid them in full on the Cross, so that leaves us with nothing but to receive His love. He is the faithful father waiting for the return of the prodigal son. He is the good shepherd that leaves the ninety-nine to go find the one that left the flock, and He is the kind-hearted Savior who saved an adulterous woman from being stoned to death, and then sent her away with His gift of no condemnation. His grace is a mystery—and it is beautiful.

This is where I started and this is where we all have to start. So, just say His name today. If you want to follow it up with prayer, that's okay. If you just want to say His name only, that's okay, too. Just say it, "Jesus." He will do the rest.

I waited patiently for the Lord; He turned to me and heard my cry. He lifted me out of the slimy pit, out of the mud and mire; He set my feet on a rock, and gave me a firm place to stand. He put a new song in my mouth, a hymn of praise to our God. Many will see and fear and put their trust in the LORD. (Psalm 40:1-3, NIV)

CHAPTER TWO

The Judge, the Attorney, and the Prosecutor

The sidewalks were one solid, moving mass of people. Television crews, cameramen, reporters, and crowds of observers pushed against each other as a white, four-door sedan pulled to the curb. The crowd quickly shifted to the passenger side door of the car and anxiously waited for the occupants to exit. A door opened and a woman's leg emerged from the car. The crowd immediately pressed in, making it difficult for the woman to open the door completely. As she attempted to exit the car to the sidewalk, the surge of the crowd almost pushed her backwards. Soon, familiar arms were around her, as the driver, who was her Attorney, rushed around the car and used his own arms and body to shield her from the crowd. As she regained her footing, he motioned for the crowd to give them room. They hesitated, but eventually obeyed. He then took her arm and they walked together to the courthouse.

It was the second week of trial and this case had become the most exciting thing this dull town had seen, other than the annual rodeo. The town's people led idle lives and a good trial was just the entertainment they needed to take them away from their own dreary lives. Her Attorney had never lost a case, so the curiosity of the locals intensified while some even placed bets on the outcome of the trial.

The defendant was nothing more than a local girl. A single mother aged thirty-five, with a bit of a sordid past. She had lived in this town all her life, married her high school sweetheart, and had two children. But a happy home, it was not. Amazingly, the marriage survived twelve years but unfaithfulness had occurred, and ended the marriage without a protest from either spouse. After her divorce, she was forced to return to the workforce, as a sales clerk in a local department store.

Things were not easy. She struggled to pay bills and fought constantly with her ex-husband about the kids. She began to seek a release from the worry and pain and that was when she began to find herself involved in things that she would not normally do. It started out with some harmless "girls night out" weekends, but eventually became a crazy rollercoaster ride of lovers and shameful activities. In just a few short months, she had completely ruined her reputation and it seemed impossible that it could ever be repaired. The more she came to this realization, the more she sank into despair, depression, and guilt.

Guilt completely dominated her life. Every time she looked at her children, she wondered if she had ruined their lives, too. Every moment she spent with her parents, she wondered if she had caused them shame. Every time she waited on a customer at the department store, she wondered if they had any knowledge of her activities. Were they talking about her? Sometimes she thought she heard her name whispered behind her back in public places and as her imagination ran rampant, she could not escape it.

There was no peace for her, even at her church. When people greeted her in the hallways, she was wary of their smiles and continually second-guessed the way they looked at her. Were they also talking about her?

It seemed that her accusers were everywhere—pointing, laughing, and judging without compassion. She wanted to run away, move to a new town, and start all over ... but what about the kids? She couldn't take them from their friends and family, and she didn't have the finances to start new anywhere else. She was stuck and wanted to die.

Now, here she was a public spectacle being judged by a jury of her peers, and on trial for her mistakes and sins. She had committed many sins and she was certain that the Prosecutor could produce mountains of damning evidence. In this town, it would not be hard to find witnesses for the prosecution. Everyone wanted their fifteen minutes of fame, and would volunteer to condemn anyone, if it meant attention and press. In a way, she felt pity for them because they were so hollow. She knew that for some of them, this town would be all they would ever experience. They would never get out of their shallow thinking and petty lives. She at least knew that if she survived this trial, and was somehow set free, she could still have a life and would do everything she could to make the most of it.

As everyone settled into the courtroom, she sat at the defendant's table and looked straight ahead. She did not want to see the eyes of her accuser. Everyone stood to their feet as the Judge approached the bench and after a few opening remarks, the trial commenced.

Since this was week two of the trial, the prosecution had already presented most of its case. There was only one person left to sit in the witness stand—the accused. As her name was called, she rose from the defendant's table and made her way to the stand. She sat facing the courtroom. As the Prosecutor approached her, he looked at her through narrowed eyes with one corner of his mouth turned slightly upwards in a subtle smirk. He meant business. His goal was to punish her, put her away for a very long time, and make her children motherless. There was no mercy in his heart and the thought of humiliating her only delighted him. His tactics were ruthless, and he had been known to reduce defendants into weeping heaps of defeat. His charming demeanor and delicate seduction of the jury clouded the courtroom with a faint sense of evil. He gave one last glance toward the defendant's table, smiled at the defense Attorney, and turned to the witness stand to begin his questioning.

"Having a good day?" he sneered.

Her voice was barely audible, "Yes."

"Speak loudly!" he said abruptly. "The whole court needs to hear your answers."

"Yes." Her voice was shaking.

"I've been told that you claim to be a Christian. Is this true?" he sneered.

She swallowed hard and answered, "Yes."

He snapped, "Then Christians normally lie, cheat, and indulge in sexual immorality?"

"They shouldn't, but ..."

He interrupted loudly, "But what? Isn't it against God's law? Do you remember the Ten Commandments or shall I review them?"

Her chin began to quiver, "Yes, I remember." Her voice was a whisper. She looked at the faces around the courtroom for needed support. As she scanned the room, she glanced toward the defendant's table and locked eyes with her Attorney. There was peace in those eyes. She could get lost in them and for a moment, she did. He smiled at her and her heart was revived with hope.

Weeks earlier when she had realized that she was in trouble and in need of defense, she called him. When she met him, she was so weak with distress and pain she could do nothing but sit before him and cry. In broken sentences she sobbed, "I've made such a mess ... I'm so sorry." His eyes were full of compassion for her and for the first time in her life, she saw love—real, unconditional love. He gently held out his hand and said, "You're forgiven. Will you trust me?"

Memories were swirling around in her head as the activities of the courtroom faded in and out. She didn't even notice the Prosecutor raising his voice to her.

"I repeat! Do you know the Ten Commandments and haven't you broken them?" The Prosecutor's face was turning red.

With her eyes still magnetized to the face of her Attorney, she softly spoke under her breath, "I trust you."

The Prosecutor angrily scowled, "Your honor, since the subject cannot even participate in an intelligible conversation, I would like to submit to the court Exhibit A."

One of the Prosecutor's assistants nervously approached the bench with a large envelope. The assistant opened the envelope and attempted to pour the contents onto a table. He shook the envelope vigorously, but nothing came out. He looked into the envelope, then back at the Prosecutor, bewildered. With a bit of embarrassment, the Prosecutor asked the Judge for a moment to sort through the confusion. The Judge nodded.

The assistant was sent to fetch another envelope. He returned with another and the same thing happened, the envelope was empty. More assistants brought envelopes, boxes, cassette cases, and all of them were empty.

Furious, the Prosecutor spun around to face the defendant's Attorney. "You've tampered with my evidence!"

The defending Attorney calmly rose from his seat and asked, "Your Honor, may I approach the bench?"

"Of course you may," was the reply.

Her Attorney was gentle as a dove, yet had a strong air of wisdom and authority. As he walked towards the Judge's bench, every eye was on him. They could not look away. There was something alluring, something beautiful about him. He was simply mesmerizing. He gazed at the Judge with a look of familiarity and one could see that they knew each other. As he drew nearer, he looked at the accused and said softly, "Hold your head up. You have nothing to be ashamed of."

He stood before the Judge and spoke clearly, "Your Honor, there is no evidence against this dear woman today and there *never* will be evidence against her because it does not exist. There are no records against her and her sins are as far removed as the east is from the west. Her slate is clean."

The Prosecutor stomped his foot and screamed, "But Your Honor, we have witnesses!" He turned to the courtroom and threw his voice across the audience of spectators. "People of the courtroom, this woman has done terrible things, things that *you* would never do." A few people in the audience began to squirm uncomfortably in their seats, as conviction seemed to hover over the courtroom. "Isn't there anyone here that will attest to the fact that she should be punished?"

The defense Attorney turned to face the crowd. "Anyone?"

Every mouth was silent. No one dared speak.

The Attorney turned back to the Judge and gently spoke, "There are no records against her. She must be pronounced 'Not guilty.'"

The Judge looked at the defendant and asked her, "How do you plead?"

She looked around the room and then into the eyes of her Attorney and confidently said, "Not guilty!"

The gavel came down as the Judge loudly proclaimed, "*Not guilty!*"

The Prosecutor glared at her Attorney and with a growl in his voice, he arrogantly sneered, "Next time." He walked away defeated.

Her Attorney reached out his hand to help her from the witness stand. She was speechless. He was the one that broke the silence. He only spoke three words, but they were the best words she had ever heard in her life. "You are free!"

Who is the woman in this story? She is me and she is you. The Attorney is Jesus and He sits in Heaven right now defending you day and night from the Accuser of the Brethren, who has it in for you. But if you have made mistakes and you have honestly asked the Lord to forgive you, then you have no more reason to feel guilty about anything. Jesus has conquered the devil and the grave to make you free. He did not hang on a Cross for six hours in agony, suffering rejection and making a spectacle of the Devil so that you can wallow in guilt for the rest of your life. You have been granted freedom, so live like it. Grace is yours—reach out and take it. Every time any reminder of your mistakes tries to present itself, declare yourself "Not guilty." You are free!

Because the Sovereign LORD helps me, I will not be disgraced. Therefore I have set my face like flint, And I know I will not be put to shame. He who vindicates me is near. Who then will bring charges against me? Let us face each other! Who is my accuser? Let him confront me! It is the Sovereign LORD who helps me. Who is he that will condemn me? (Isaiah 50:7-9, NIV)

CHAPTER THREE

Leah's Honeymoon

The very first time I attended a divorce recovery workshop as a new participant, I was newly separated, and, as I said before, I was already dating. I considered myself a pro at dating since I had dated several men before I met my husband and had received several marriage proposals. Getting back on the dating bus did not intimidate me at all and I was full of confidence and feminine determination. At that time, I thought it was power.

My attitudes about dating had been formed from the time I was in my early teens, from peers, TV, magazines, and books. They all said the same thing: don't "give it up" on the first date or you will appear easy, then when you really love someone, it's okay. As you continue into a long relationship, the romance and pretensions start to fade as the relationship heads in the direction of commitment. After a while, you get engaged, fight a little (or a lot) and as the wedding night approaches, you refrain from sex for a few weeks so your wedding night will be "special." Give or take a few minor changes and details, that is the experience and attitude of most of the American public. I knew it all, so a divorce recovery workshop didn't really need to teach me how to snag a man. Yet, that night I met a woman who threw me for a loop.

Leah was very beautiful and had a positive energy about her. She was one of the facilitators who had a wonderful story of grace and restoration. After having divorced three years earlier, she had recently married the man of her dreams so she was still on the honeymoon high. I had a desire to remarry, too, so I wanted to quiz her on how she accomplished landing a great husband. She was eager to tell me her story.

She, like many others, had rushed into the dating scene immediately after her divorce and exposed herself to compromising situations. Because she was still dealing with issues from her divorce, she found herself acting out and doing things that were uncharacteristic for her. Since she was still active at her church, she was finding that the inner conflict and guilt of her secret lifestyle were taking a toll on her. She made a brave decision to give it over to the Lord and to wait for His direction in her life.

Within months, a long-time male friend began spending time with her. He was a strong Christian and although he was well into his late twenties, he had remained pure and was saving himself for marriage. As they grew closer together, the perpetual question in Leah's heart was, "Why would he want me when I'm damaged goods?"

It turned out that he was a gentleman, loved God, and he did want her—just the way she was. Their relationship continued in an honorable way and they got married.

This next part is where she really grabbed my attention. She was glowing and could not hold back how wonderful their wedding night was. I'm not kidding—she was radiant. Out of her exuberance, she was gushing details that might make some people blush! The whole point was, she had never felt so treasured and special and all because he had respected her enough to wait. These two people experienced something very few people do these days; they remained pure until their wedding night and the reward was completely exciting and exhilarating!

"Wow!" I thought to myself. That sure challenges our modern day view of courtship and marriage. In our society, everyone believes you have to make sure you are sexually compatible with someone *before* you marry. How can you make sure a shoe fits if you don't try it on? Shouldn't you taste the milk before you buy the cow? What do you do for those long months before you're married? Bible studies over the phone?

Even to me, the notion of staying completely pure until the wedding night was a little unrealistic. I lived in the real world. Now, I had known many Christians who managed to save the actual sexual act for their wedding night, but had experimented and done just about everything else beforehand. That prospect fit a little more within my realm of reality. But total restraint? The thought of absolute abstinence, especially when you have been married and have had total access to all the sex you want, seemed like taking twenty steps backwards and falling off a cliff.

But it stuck in my mind. God stuck it there. For the next few weeks, I began playing out in my mind how it would feel to be treated respectfully by a man who had *my* honor and *his* commitment to God as his top priorities?. Intriguing. I had to admit that sitting across a table from men who were having conversations with the top two buttons of my blouse was getting old. And I certainly didn't want to be one of those moms whose children had a lot of "uncles" in and out of their lives.

However, that age-old question kept circling through my mind. "What if you married the guy and, it wasn't what you had hoped for?" Isn't sex the most important thing? Of course, I could answer that question easily. I have met people that were still sexually active with their spouses up until the night before their spouse filed for divorce, so sex is not the thing that keeps marriages together.

I began to picture in my mind the guy who, after a date, politely saw me to the door and returned me to my sons unharmed and uncompromised. I could almost feel that clean feeling of having fun and pure dates with someone who is my best friend. And I had always wanted to date a man who truly loved church and ministry as much as I did and didn't groan over the thought of going to services *again*. I was beginning to visualize and desire the kind of wedding night that very few people on this Earth have. The kind of wedding night that God designed. I wanted things to be different this time. I wanted to be cherished and honored and desired. I wanted what Leah had!

I prayed, thought it over and prayed some more. It all boiled down to one question: Did I trust God enough to give everything, even my love life and marriage, over to Him? If I trusted God enough to give me a great man who loved Him, and that I could be compatible with, couldn't God also make sure that we would be compatible in the other departments too? In His own words, here is His reply to that question, found in Psalm 37:4, NIV: *"Delight yourself in the LORD and he will give you the desires of your heart."* Today, dream big. Let your mind explore the possibilities. Could how you do things be different this time? They say that if you keep doing the same things, you will keep getting the same results. So what if you do things *differently* this time? What if, like Leah did, you turn it all over to God and He surprises you with something new you never dreamed of? If He did it for her, He will do it for you. "All things are possible to them that believe."

> *Therefore I am now going to allure her; I will lead her into the desert and speak tenderly to her.*
>
> *There I will give her back her vineyards, and I will make the Valley of Achor [trouble], a door of hope. There she will sing as in the days of her youth.* (Hosea 2:14-15, NIV)

CHAPTER FOUR

Get Out the Artillery

King Jehoshaphat was finishing breakfast as his servant was clearing dishes away from the table. As she reached to take his cup, he smiled and spoke softly, "I'm going to sip on that a little longer." It was a beautiful morning and the King was in good spirits.

King Jehoshaphat's palace was located in Jerusalem, in the land of Judah, which was powerful and for the most part peaceful at that time. As he held his cup and thoughtfully gazed out the window, one of his advisors seated at the other end of the table going over the day's schedule was about to speak but stopped short when a soldier appeared in the doorway with a grave look on his face.

"What is it?" King Jehoshaphat asked the soldier.

"There's a messenger," he replied, "and he has urgent news, Sire."

"Send him in," King Jehoshaphat commanded as he and his advisor exchanged glances, neither knowing what it could possibly be.

The messenger stumbled through the door, slightly crouched over, gasping, and unable to catch his breath. He was drenched in sweat, shaky and troubled. He took a long swallow and cried out, "A vast army is coming against you from Edom, allies from the other side of the sea. They are already in Hazazon Tamar."

Alarmed, the King and his advisor jumped to their feet with looks of consternation on their faces. King Jehoshaphat, responding quickly, told the messenger to go and get the priest. Then he ordered an immediate assembly of the people to proclaim a fast for all Judah.

The messenger left with his new mission and the advisor quickly left with his own set of details to tend to. King Jehoshaphat, now alone in the room, slowly sat back down in his chair. He looked back out the window briefly then put his head in his hands and rubbed his face as if to erase the last few moments. He was severely distraught because this could only mean one thing: if God did not intervene, Jerusalem would be no more.

Within a short time, throngs of people had come from all parts of Judah to seek the Lord and hear from King Jehoshaphat. They all congregated in front of the Temple of the Lord where the king and all his officials waited to address the crowd. King Jehoshaphat arose and the crowd was hushed as every eye looked at him. Then King Jehoshaphat stepped forward and as he turned his face upward, he began to speak in a powerful voice, "O Lord, God of our fathers, are you not the God who is in Heaven? You rule over all the kingdoms of the nations. Power and might are in your hand and no one can withstand you."

As he spoke, the people were amazed at his assurance. He was a great king and sounded confident as he addressed God in His great Throne Room above. He prayed for several minutes, and then closed his prayer by saying, "We have no power to face this vast army that is attacking us. We do not know what to do, but our eyes are upon you."

There was a moment of silence, and then one of the men in the assembly, Jahaziel, stood up and, through the Spirit of the Lord, spoke. "This is what the Lord says: 'Do not be afraid or discouraged, for the battle is not yours, but God's. Go out to face them tomorrow and the Lord will be with you.'"

Some men in the front of the crowd began praising the Lord with loud voices and slowly others began to join in. A spirit of victory took over as their raised voices were heard throughout the countryside. Fear could not survive in a crowd like that, for they were not trying to stir up courage before a battle; they were already proclaiming the victory! Their enemies had already been slain. It was as good as done.

The next morning Jehoshaphat gave orders as to how the army would be assembled. The front lines were the most important and his strategy was one of solid faith. He assembled the heaviest artillery to march out before the army—a choir! Not a choir armed with swords, or spears, but armed with voices of thanks and praise. He gave the command and as the army moved out, the choir began singing, "Give thanks to the Lord, for His love endures forever!"

As they began to sing, the Lord started fighting for them causing the enemy allies to turn on each other in confusion.

In their frightened state, the allies destroyed each other until none was left. By the time King Jehoshaphat and his army arrived at the battlefield, there was nothing left but dead bodies, and a lot of plunder. They returned to Jerusalem joyful and carrying the valuables left from their enemies. There was no doubt in their minds that they had witnessed a supernatural event. Jerusalem had been saved, not by swords and spears, but by a God who was moved by their faith, praise, and thanks.

So let's put this in today's terms. How does this apply to you? Every morning when you get up, as you are getting dressed for the day and eating breakfast, an army is assembling outside your front door. It's an army of enemies who have allied against you. These armies are depression, self-hatred, fear, unforgiveness, anger, passiveness, lust, doubt, and many others. They are confidently waiting for you to take your first steps into the day. Their plan is to ambush and defeat you.

Picture this: This army is waiting for you in your front yard, checking the points on their spears, tightening their sword belts, and joking with one another when the door cracks open. They quickly assume an offensive position and lower their brows. Grrrrrrr . . . they are ready for you.

Quick as a flash, their plans are dashed as you step out onto the porch with a smile on your face and proclaim loudly, "Thank You, Lord, for all your blessings today!"

"Huh?"

One of the army captains slaps another on the head and says, "I thought you said she would be easy! She's got the Lord fighting for her!" The army begins nervously looking around. A spirit of fear and terror arises among them and pandemonium breaks out. In their confusion, they turn on each other and begin destroying one another. In a moment, it is all over. By the time you step off the porch toward your car, there are dead bodies all around.

Does that really happen? Maybe not *exactly* as I described it, but the Bible is a spiritual book and there is no doubt that there is a spiritual lesson here. There's a battle going on for your life and your future and you had better have the right ammunition to defeat your enemy or you will be defeated.

In the morning as you get dressed for the day and drive to work, what is on your mind? What's on the radio? (Please don't tell me you listen to songs that bring back sad memories or stir you up sexually. Turn off the radio!) Every morning, I want you to say aloud, five things that you are thankful for. Remember, we are reprogramming your mind. What you did last week will not work anymore. You may not feel like giving thanks, but you must. This will be your artillery for the day and in the coming weeks as we're reshaping your heart for a new vision. Here's a sample of some of my thanksgivings:

1) I am thankful that I'm a mother. Watching my sons play baseball is Heaven on Earth!

2) I am thankful for my best friend, Kim. She knows every bad thing I have ever done and she *still* loves me!

3) I am thankful I could afford coffee and eggs for breakfast. Some people never know that luxury.

4) I am thankful I was raised in church. Church camps are my fondest memories. It made me who I am today.

5) I am thankful for my little dog—he makes me laugh because he's a Chihuahua who thinks he's a Pit Bull.

Learning to thank God in the good and the bad times was the single most important spiritual weapon the Lord gave me. It was the first lesson He taught me about healing after my divorce and it has set the tone for the rest of the journey into my future. No matter what state we find ourselves in—married, divorced, or single-hoping-to-be-married-someday, we have to learn to be content and thankful for our present situation. The Apostle Paul admonished us many times to give thanks because it teaches us to keep our eyes on all the good gifts God gives us daily and keeps us from meditating on the negatives in our lives. Not only that, it unlocks spiritual doors in our lives that allow God to work on our behalf. This is crucial for you as a single person. Remember, do not be afraid or discouraged, for the battle is not yours, but God's.

Just a few days ago, while out for my evening walk, I caught myself starting to meditate on my problems. Putting this principal to work, I immediately opened my mouth and started singing aloud an old hymn I used to sing as a child, "Count Your Blessings." Within minutes my mind was eased and the power of praise renewed my strength and trust in God.

Praise and thanksgivings are powerful weapons. It may not make sense to us sometimes but it makes a huge difference in the spiritual because it will eventually manifest in the natural. Commit to this way and you will win your battles from now on. Not by worrying, or taking things into your own hands, but by trusting that your God is all-powerful and no enemy can stand against Him.

Put Your Past to Rest and Move On

Though no one can go back and make a

brand new start, anyone can start from now

and make a brand new ending.

— CARL BARD

CHAPTER FIVE

The Ball and Chain

Marty sat at his desk staring out the window. He had just finished a sandwich for lunch and the afternoon drowsies were coming upon him. There were stacks of unfinished paperwork on his desk, but as he gazed out into the street, he wanted to take a few minutes to enjoy his favorite pastime—people watching. His office was located on the ground floor of his building in a busy business district and there was always a steady flow of people on the sidewalks. His eyes sorted through the crowds to pick an interesting subject. There were plenty of opportunities within the crowds of people.

A man passed by that Marty assumed was homeless. He carried a plastic bag with what looked like his only possessions and his eyes peered out of a face framed by a long, scraggly beard that draped down over his dirty clothes. As most people watchers do, Marty became a little emotional as he imagined that this was someone's father or brother. He watched until the man was out of sight.

Marty scanned the sidewalks searching for another interesting person. There was a mom with two children, one was crying. Behind her was an older, balding man. A few steps behind him walked a woman he estimated to be in her fifties. Squinting his eyes, he leaned closer to the window; it was a woman with ... something on her left foot. Marty jumped to his feet saying under his breath, "What in the world?"

The woman was walking down the street with a ball and chain around her ankle! Was she an escaped convict? Not by the way she was dressed. His face was almost pressed to the window. She dragged her left foot slowly as it labored under the weight of the ball. Her eyes looked straight ahead, but her face did not indicate that she was in any distressed situation and she greeted others as they passed her by. They didn't even acknowledge the ball and chain on her foot. Everyone acted normally. This was crazy! Who was this woman?

Curiosity was coursing through his veins. He arose and swiftly walked through the office to the front door. "Glenda, hold my calls," he puffed as he went out the door.

The woman was still in view and he walked over to the newspaper stand next door to question the owner, who was standing out on the sidewalk. "See that woman with the ball and chain? Do you know who she is?"

The man spun around toward the street, anxious to add a little excitement to his day. "Which one?" he asked.

Marty was puzzled. He pointed, "That woman right there! The one with the ball and chain on her foot."

"I see the woman, but I don't see a ball and chain on either of her feet," the shop owner responded.

Marty looked around quickly and stopped a passerby, another man. "Do you see the ball and chain on that woman's foot?"

The man turned his head toward the street and studied intently for a moment. He turned back to Marty. "I see lots of women, but no one with a ball and chain. Is this a joke?"

Marty was bewildered. There was only one thing to do: go straight to the source. By this time the woman was a block away and Marty half-walked, half-ran to catch up to her. The whole time he was thinking in his head, "Exactly what am I going to say to her?"

When he caught up to her, he took a good look at her feet. There was no doubt—that was a ball and chain. Breathlessly, he tapped her on the sleeve and in a disbelieving tone said, "Ma'am, am I correctly seeing a ball and chain on your left ankle?"

"Oh, you can see it? Not everyone can, but some do." She responded as she slowly walked on.

This was the twilight zone! There was no other explanation. But he had to press on; this was too good.

"May I ask why you have it?"

Now she stopped walking and faced him. "I just woke up one morning and it was there. It is on there for good. See that name on it?"

He bent down to find a name written on the ball. "Tammy?" he half whispered.

"Yes, Tammy," she said with a serious undertone. "Tammy is the name of the tramp who stole my husband. I hate her! She took everything I ever loved and my family is now gone. A few weeks after she took my husband, I called her at her job to confront her. I actually thought she might be sorry for tearing my family apart. What a laugh! She told me I should have taken better care of my husband and he wouldn't have had to go to her for attention. I told her I would never forgive her and I never will! The next morning I woke up and this ball and chain was around my ankle. It has been there ever since. I cannot do anything without this reminder of her. When I go to bed at night, it keeps me awake. The next morning, it is the first thing I see. Every time I turn around, it reminds me of her!"

Marty was amazed. "So other people have noticed it too?"

"Some. It seems to be invisible, except to people that know me. Last week, I went on a blind date. Everything seemed to be going fine, but at dinner, I guess maybe I talked about my ex-husband and Tammy too much. My date looked down for a moment then looked at me a little embarrassed. I then realized he had noticed the ball and chain. He cut the evening short and I haven't seen him since. I really hate this thing. As soon as people see it, they get really uncomfortable and act like they don't want to be around me anymore."

Marty, perceiving the situation asked, "Do you think the ball and chain and you're unwillingness to forgive Tammy could be related? I mean, it *did* appear after you said you would never forgive her."

"Oh, I'm sure of it. I have carried this thing around for two years. I've done a lot of thinking about it and I'm sure it's there because of my unforgiveness."

"So why don't you just forgive her?"

The woman sadly shook her head. Her voice was low. "No, I can't. It will make what she did okay and it is not okay."

"Well, does she know that you're carrying this around?"

"Nope, I doubt she even cares. She's too busy running around to parties with my husband"

Marty was full of compassion for this woman. The answer was so clear to him and he wanted to help her break free of this thing. "Ma'am, it's clear that the only person this is hurting is you. I bet if you forgive her, the ball and chain will be gone and you will be free of it. Why don't you just try?"

The woman changed her countenance and the corners of her mouth shifted downward. She looked away from Marty toward the direction she had been walking. She was through talking to him. He was just like everyone else. Clearly, he did not understand. She took a step and strained a little as the ball began to give its weight to move with her foot. She said one last thing as she walked away. "I'll never forgive her."

Marty stood on the sidewalk and watched her walk away, dragging the load behind her. He could hear the chain jingle with every step. The name *Tammy* was visible on the ball as it moved slowly out of sight. For a second, he couldn't move, then he mechanically turned back in the direction of his office and started walking, hardly noticing the people passing him. A slight tear formed in his eye as he realized the full impact of what he had just seen. After a moment, he heard a familiar jingle and looked across the street in the direction of the sound. He saw a young man walking slowly, slightly limping. There was a ball and chain around his ankle.

I am sure the moral of this story is quite evident: when we hate someone and won't forgive him or her, we are actually attaching ourselves to the very person we don't like. Unforgiveness is not an emotion; it is a spiritual force. It is so strong that Jesus said it keeps our prayers from being heard. If it were not a big deal, God would not have bothered mentioning it, but He *did* mention it several times. This is big to Him.

Why? Because He came to set you free! This thing is enslaving you and He cannot just let you walk away without trying to help you. He cares, and you're His child, for goodness sake! He wants to see you laugh and He wants to take you to His favorite places. He wants you to run, skip, and act silly. Then He wants to see you fall asleep at night with a smile on your face. As long as you are holding a grudge against someone, these things cannot happen in your life.

Are you carrying around a ball and chain with someone's name on it? Stop now and take a good look. Please do not walk away dragging that thing behind you, get it off! If you're waiting for that person who hurt you to apologize, you may be waiting for the rest of your life. They may *never* apologize. They may be able to sleep at night comfortably, without a thought about how they hurt you. God knows that. It's *you* He's chasing.

He's got the key to the ball and chain. Luke 6:37, NIV: "... *forgive and you will be forgiven.*" It is not rocket science. Just tell Jesus you forgive them. Done—ball and chain gone. Don't let the devil tell you it's not that easy. He wants you to stumble over this and he whispers to you that you should wait until you *feel* like doing it. He wants you to drag it around for the rest of your life because he loves to look around and see all the people dragging balls and chains. He gets a kick out of it.

Please, please allow God to transform you into a forgiving person. Forgive those who have done a tremendous injustice to you. Forgive those who accidentally put their foot in their mouths, and, forgive those who do not even know they hurt you. This is so important. How can you move forward in a new relationship with a ball and chain attached to yourself? Do you think that new person in your life will never see it? Take care of it now. Put the book down. Go talk to Jesus.

CHAPTER SIX

Hummingbirds

I have a friend named George. He is a single, divorced man who has been a strong leader and facilitator in our divorce recovery program at my church. He was divorced four years ago and has grown spiritually by leaps and bounds as God transforms him during this special time of singleness. We are building a website designed for divorced and single adults, so we talk frequently and usually end up sharing the new revelations that God is showing us. He got me tickled one day as he told me about a funny, but profound, incident that had happened earlier that morning.

George had become accustomed to having daily, morning devotions in his garage with the door open so that he could enjoy the newness of the day. That morning as he began reading, a hummingbird flew into the garage and after a few moments, it was apparent that it could not find its way out. The bird fruitlessly bumped around the walls of the garage, and George's soft heart was stirred with true concern. He knew that it was time to put on his superhero cape and save the day.

He got up from his chair and began to pursue the bird in an attempt to direct him toward freedom. A few swipes in the air indicated that simply waving his hands around did nothing but confuse the poor little thing. The bird became frightened and flew away from him. If the bird got close to the opening of the garage, George would try to swish him out, but the crazy thing would actually fly back into the garage beyond George's reach. George then decided that he needed the help of a broom. I could easily picture the looks on the faces of his neighbors as they saw him in his garage running around swinging a broom. He was getting frustrated as he thought, "Can't this bird see that I'm trying to help him?" After several minutes of swinging, poking, and guiding, the bird finally flew out of the garage into the open air. Whew!

As George took his seat to resume his meditations, God was clearly using what had just happened to teach him something. Sometimes we are stuck in a rut and God is trying to guide us out but we don't recognize it. We are just like that little bird that is frantically trying to find the way out, desperately looking for an escape, and yet getting nowhere. We keep running around in circles bumping into walls as God is waving His hands trying to show us the way to freedom.

There are a lot of different kinds of ruts that can trap us. I see a lot of anger, bitterness, and unforgiveness in divorced people, but I have observed a particular rut that seems to have a strong hold on people, keeping them in bondage for months and years at a time. That rut is negative and obsessive thinking. I am speaking of people like you and me that engage in a cycle of destructive thoughts repeatedly, day in and day out—thoughts that keep us stuck in a place from which we cannot find the way out. They are thoughts that we express out loud over and over to anyone who will listen, eventually driving people away.

It is very easy to detect someone who is stuck in a cycle of thoughts. It's the only thing they talk about. Nothing is more unappealing than someone who talks about his or her ex constantly, or those who constantly dredge up past experiences in which they were wronged, cheated, or hurt. It controls them and it's on their minds from sunup to sundown. It is terribly addictive behavior that becomes a part of the person. They cannot stop. It's like a high that gives them a surge of endorphins every time they tell the story. It gives them validity, sympathy, attention, and satisfaction. It is their new lover. I know; I used to be that person.

Stopping the patterns of negative and obsessive thoughts is not easy. When your thoughts—and words—have been allowed to roam free, trying to corral them is like trying to catch fifty hummingbirds frantically flying around in a garage. If you are going to catch them, you had better saddle up with a lot of determination.

First, you have to realize one thing. Saying something over and over in your mind, or out loud, keeps it alive. It gives it life and breath every time you allow it to revisit your mind. It keeps the past around and it energizes your emotions toward that subject. It is like giving it a vitamin every day to keep it thriving. It is powerful, it is real, and its bitterness can eventually kill you spiritually, and even physically.

The tongue has the power of life and death, and those who love it will eat its fruit. (Proverbs 18:21, NIV)

I heard some interesting statistics yesterday. Seventy-seven percent of the thoughts that a person thinks or meditates on during a twenty-four hour period are negative, *and* for every five minutes of negative thought that you engage in, your body counteractively suffers twenty-four hours for that thought. No wonder people have ulcers! Even secular authors, counselors, and specialists all agree on one thing: your belief system and your thoughts will dictate your life.

Today is the day you take back your mind. Your mind is not for sale. God gave it to you to protect, maintain, educate, and use for His glory. Unfortunately, there is someone else who also sees the value of your mind and he wants to make it useless, stale, and captive. But I don't like to campaign for him. Who is he anyway? Jesus made a spectacle of him thousands of years ago on the Cross when He overcame him and crushed his head. So now you, strengthened through Christ, can easily defeat him too. I would advise that you openly, out loud, take your mind back for yourself and for Christ. Then you will need to do some serious follow-up.

Sometimes those tapes that play over and over in our minds seem to play on autopilot, playing for minutes or hours before we even realize what has taken place. Although you have been enlightened about their destruction and have made a commitment to stop them, it takes some strong measures to shut them down.

First of all, you will need to identify the times of day that your mind is idle and your thoughts take off. For me, those times are in the morning when I'm putting on my makeup, when I'm driving, and a few other monotonous activities that seem to cause me to zone out. You need to be prepared to have good replacement thoughts in place and ready to go. We don't want those destructive thoughts to have a chance.

When I am getting ready in the mornings, I get out a CD and play it while I get ready. I am partial to uplifting Christian music or CD's of my preacher and other great speakers who have godly wisdom. If I am on a trip, I turn on the television and find a good Christian program, but I rarely allow dead silence in my idle times unless I am specifically in prayer and waiting on God. I also keep Scriptures close by that I am trying to memorize. I tape them to my mirror, keep them in my car, and I have two of them taped to my computer screen at this very moment while I am writing this book. It has slowly become a habit and a drive of mine to protect my mind and not allow it to roam.

Remember, we want your replacement thoughts to be uplifting, promising, wholesome, and straight from God. Did you know that you could set the tone for your thought life for the whole day by preparing the night before? Studies have shown that the things you take into your mind the last forty-five minutes of the day, before you retire to sleep, are what you bring into your reality. This was extremely eye-opening for me because I used to love to watch those creepy, forensic shows as I was nodding off to sleep. You know, the ones where they show photos of dead people and then spend the rest of the show following up on the clues, the killer, and gathering the evidence. God set me straight on that. There's not anything wrong with those shows but it is definitely not the place to find your *new* thoughts when you are in a time of healing.

Read the whole Book of Proverbs. Even if you have read it before, read it this time with the goal of gaining wisdom, teaching your mind proper thoughts and actions, and learning the heart of God. The Book of Psalms is also a wonderful place to develop new thoughts and learn what God's thoughts are. The Psalms are also meant to teach you about spiritual warfare. When you begin to memorize the words and speak them out loud, they become your bows and arrows, going before you and accomplishing the purpose God set forth for them. They are incredibly powerful and will always accomplish His will since they do not return to Him without fulfilling their purpose.

I find the book of Psalms a treasure chest full of useful spiritual weapons. There have been many times when faced with a dire situation, I have walked around my house with my Bible open reading Psalm 18 out loud. I have experienced some wonderful results from this gift that God has given us.

So from now, on no more negative or obsessive thoughts. This will be such an asset to the one that you date and marry. Your words of life and encouragement will minister to that person and bring love and goodness to your relationship. The time to learn this is now so that it becomes second nature to you.

I am already excited about the person that is going to get to marry you! They are going to get a real treasure, someone that is balanced, wise, and knows how to trust the Lord at all times. Your thoughts and words of wisdom are going to be such a blessing to that person that they will feel they have found a pot of gold!

CHAPTER SEVEN

Fatherless Memories

If you were raised with a devoted father in the home you are very fortunate. However, many people do not know what it feels like to sit on daddy's lap and cuddle and a great many others don't have childhood memories of a warm, loving, unconditional relationship with their father (or mother). Unfortunately, this loss can transfer unhealthy views of the way we think of our Heavenly Father. It is something that has to be corrected in order for us to move forward in our walk with the Lord. How can we commune properly with Him with a faulty view of who He really is?

My father ran from the Lord for most of my childhood and his spiritual condition wreaked havoc on our family. He was rarely home and even lived in other states when I was a child. When he was home, he drank a lot and caused a lot of chaos in our family. I still have vivid memories of seeing my mother cry over my dad and wishing I was big enough to help her. My sister was my best friend and confidant as the circumstances drew us closer together.

My parents eventually ended up divorcing and my father left our home for good when I was ten. My mother remained strong throughout all of the hardships with my father and consistently kept my sister and me in church. I am full of appreciation and honor for her. She married again, this time choosing a good man who is "Grandpa" to my kids today and is beloved not only by our family but by our whole community.

When I was sixteen, my father had a miraculous encounter with God and started seeking Him with all his heart. His testimony became known throughout Christian circles, for it was a powerful one. It was wonderful seeing this man re-created into a humble, God serving preacher who eventually pastored a small church. By this time, however, he was remarried and had another family. We lived in the same town and I saw him frequently. His door was always open to me and he tried as hard as he could to restore those lost years of my childhood, many times expressing his regret through tears. We knew that we could not go back, we could only move forward, and so we did.

My father died ten years ago. In the years before he died, he had become a wise, Bible-loving man. You could ask him any question about the Bible and he knew the answer. He completely wore out five Bibles in fifteen years of study. He couldn't get enough. That was the legacy he left me: a man who spent years away from God, running and hardening his heart, finally said "Yes" to God, and turned into a kind, happy preacher with friends and family who loved him.

Yet, I was left with a big *why?* in my heart. Why couldn't he have changed earlier, *before* my parents divorced? I had spent years wishing my sister and I could have had him consistently as a dedicated father throughout all the stages of growth in our lives. It was strange at his funeral when my half-brothers made all the arrangements and I felt more like a guest than his firstborn child. I found myself grieving more over the loss of my father from when I was a child than when he actually died. At the funeral, I realized that I had really lost him in the divorce and it was never the same after that.

It was good that I was grieving. God wanted to use that grief to teach me something. The question I had been asking God—why I couldn't have had my daddy in those crucial years of my childhood, was setting the stage for something great. God had me exactly where He wanted me. I had a question and He had an answer.

He began taking me through Scripture to study those great men and women of faith that are our Christian heritage. These were men that didn't have fathers to lead them, yet became our spiritual leaders and forefathers, in spite of their upbringing. Their testimonies are powerful and encouraging. I have listed a few:

• Abraham was told by God that he must leave his father's family and go to a new place that God would tell him. Although his father had already died, he needed to emancipate himself from the pagan life in which he had been raised. He began a new walk and was chosen by God to become the father of our faith.

• Moses did not seem to have any kind of relationship with a father figure. He was raised by Pharaoh's daughter but was forced to run away to the desert after he murdered a man. His father-in-law seems to be the first man to give Moses fatherly advice. Yet, he was chosen by God to deliver the Israelites out of slavery and became the most humble man on Earth. The Bible says that God talked to him as a friend and it is clear that he experienced a closeness to God that went far above any earthly relationship he could have had.

• Joseph was cruelly ripped from his father when he was just a young teen and sold into slavery by his own brothers. (Talk about dysfunction!) He practically grew into adulthood in prison after being falsely accused of rape. But God was faithful and years later, when he was finally reunited with his father, Joseph was second in command over all of Egypt. He remained faithful to God during his heartache and even forgave his brothers for what they did. He ended up being a man of high integrity and moral character and saved a whole country from a terrible famine.

• Samuel was the son of Hannah. She was barren, but had promised God that if He would give her a son she would dedicate him to God. Hannah's plea was heard by God and she had her baby son, Samuel. As soon as he was weaned he was taken to live in the House of the Lord and Eli, the priest, raised him. He grew to be a great prophet and anointed David as King over Israel. His guidance was the instrument that ushered in the rule of a great nation. When he died, all of Israel mourned.

• Esther's mother and father died when she was a young child. Her cousin, Mordecai, adopted and raised her as his own. Despite her loss, she grew into a lovely woman with godly wisdom. The Book of Esther tells us how the young orphaned girl became a queen and saved her people from annihilation. Esther's humble beginnings as an orphaned Hebrew (a race that was being discriminated against) prove that God truly sets us apart by the attitude of our hearts and not the distinction of our family lines.

• In the New Testament, Timothy was raised by his mother and grandmother. The Apostle Paul loved him deeply and called Timothy his true son in the faith. I think God more than made up for his loss of not being raised by his father. Timothy was blessed to be taken under Paul's wing and to be loved by him as a son.

We don't know all the "inside" stories of all the saints and how they were raised, but these examples are enough for you to get the message. Having had your father (or mother) in your life some of the time, or none of the time, does not interfere with God's love for you and His plans for your life. It is wonderful to know your father and it is always God's plan for a family to stay together. A family that has stayed intact is a beautiful thing. But if that is not the way it happened for you, please don't go through your life feeling that you have been shortchanged and will be crippled as an adult. It's just not true. God will use your upbringing to mold you into what He wants you be. He will even use the negative things in your life to make you into the image of Christ. God tells us not to be idle with our time and He practices what He preaches. There are no idle, useless events in your life when you allow God to be the Lord of all. And there is nothing that can prevent God from using you in a mighty way. Absolutely nothing!

The truth is, you were never without a father in the first place. God has always been there. He is your true, eternal Father. One day as I was having my morning devotions, I looked out the window to see the little girls across the street playing together outside. I love that family. They are wonderful parents with four adorable little girls. That morning, the dad was seated in a lawn chair on the front porch while the girls zoomed up and down the sidewalk on their tricycles and bikes. God gently spoke to my heart, "Watch them, this is how I father my children."

I put my books down and looked intently out the window. Before long, one of the little girls lost control of her tricycle and took a tumble on the sidewalk. She quickly looked around for her father, and started to whimper. She didn't have to wait long. Dad had seen the mishap and was already down the steps of the porch heading toward his little girl. He gave her a quick check over, picked up the tricycle, and placed it back on the sidewalk. As she slid back over the seat, his hand gently caressed the back of her head reassuring her that she was okay. She put her feet to the pedals and was off again as he resumed his spot on the porch.

As I sat on my couch reviewing what I had just seen, it was easy to figure out what God wanted to teach me that morning. God is our Father, always watching us while we go through life, laughing, playing, getting married, having children, and He is always watching like an attentive father. Then one day, we have a mishap and find ourselves wrecked and on the side of life's road looking for our heavenly Father's help. He comes to us, picks us up, and puts us back on our way, but not without His reassurance that we will be okay. He's always there and nothing we do escapes Him. Psalm 34:15, NIV says, *"The eyes of the LORD are on the righteous and his ears are attentive to their cry."*

Listen to me, sister or brother. You will never have a mishap that God won't see and tend to. Never! He will always come to your aid when you look for Him and call out to Him. Even when your natural parents can't be there for you, He will be there. He is your *true* Father. Psalm

27:10, AMP: *"Although my father and mother have forsaken me, yet the Lord will take me up [adopt me as His child]."* Don't ever say the words, "I don't have a father." You *do* have a Father. He is a good Father. He *invented* fatherhood! He knows how to do it right and you are in good hands. I leave you with words straight from His own mouth on His view of fathering:

> *Which of you, if his son asks for bread, will give him a stone? Or if he asks for a fish, will give him a snake? If you, then, though you are evil, know how to give good gifts to your children, how much more will your Father in heaven give good gifts to those who ask him!* (Matthew 7:9-11, NIV)

CHAPTER EIGHT

No Limits, No Boundaries

This is the chapter I couldn't wait to write! I am excited as I type 200 words a minute to get it all out. (Maybe not quite 200 w.p.m., but it feels like it.) I love nature and taking in God's creation around me. Especially zoos, animals, and standing on the beach in front of an immense ocean. Many nights find me lying down on a trampoline or in my driveway looking at all the stars. My love of God is deepened; as He gives me a glimpse of *who* He is and *how* He created the Earth and the heavens by the Word of His mouth ... He is the God who can create anything!

He spreads out the northern skies over empty space; he suspends the Earth over nothing. He wraps up the waters in His clouds, yet the clouds do not burst under their weight. He covers the face of the full moon, spreading his clouds over it. He marks out the horizon on the face of the waters for a boundary between light and darkness. The pillars of the heavens quake, aghast at his rebuke.... And these are but the outer fringe of his works; How faint the whisper we

*hear of him! Who then can understand the thunder
of his power?* (Job 26:7-11,14, NIV)

Don't you just love it when scientists say that there
are still unidentified species of creatures and insects on the
Earth that we haven't discovered yet? Or, how about those
astronomers who keep finding more galaxies millions of
light years away! It reminds me of some of God's wonderful
phrases like, "Try to count the sands on the sea" or "I
know the very number of hairs on your head." Our wee
little minds cannot comprehend these things, but they are
so easy for God. "Never-ending" is a powerful word and
yet it describes all of our Father's attributes. His wisdom is
never-ending, His power is never-ending, and his mercy is
never-ending. Wow!

We live in a society that in some ways robs us of the
ability to think or believe without limits. Although we say
things like, *Anything is possible*, most people follow that
up with a statement like, *Get real!* We are permeated with
clichés such as, *Come back to reality, I won't believe it till I
see it, You can only go so far, No way! It's hopeless, We're at a
dead end, It's terminal, There's no hope*, and many others.

These phrases definitely did not come from the mouth
of God because He knows no boundaries or limits, He can
do anything. Sometimes this short-sightedness of ours leaks
into our prayer and thought lives and we just ask God for
the things our feeble minds can think of. We may believe
we are thinking big, but only God knows the multitude of
possibilities and options that are truly available to us.

This all began to weigh on me as I presented my
requests to the Lord. I felt him saying to me, "Can't you
think bigger than that? Is that all you think I can do?" I

would respond with something like, "Well, I don't want to ask for too much." It occurred to me that I wasn't treating God as the One who could do *anything*. I was treating Him like I might treat my earthly parents—like someone with limited resources, budgets, and subject to whatever mood He might be in. I wasn't treating Him like God.

I would approach Him with words like, "I wouldn't ask unless I really needed it. If you could just spare a little ..." or, "I promise I'll give something in return." I was putting Him on the same level as a human being with limits. I did not realize how much it pleases Him to have one of His children ask Him for something specific, crazy, wild, or impossible and to really *believe* that He is the One who can make the impossible come true and treat Him so. I needed to start believing that the God who so easily created the universe or human body could easily create answers to my problems! I needed to believe that He alone was my source and at His command, there were hundreds and thousands of ways that He could provide for my needs. I needed to change my thinking.

God began to show me how to believe Him without limits. I began reading Psalm 103:2-5, NIV:

> *Praise the LORD, O my soul, and forget not all his benefits—who forgives all your sins and heals all your diseases, who redeems your life from the pit and crowns you with love and compassion, who satisfies your desires with good things so that your youth is renewed like the eagle's.*

He forgives *all* my sins? Heals *all* my diseases? Every kind or variety? Anything whatsoever? Yes, He heals *all*! Any and everything, with no limits. There are no limits with God. No limits to how much He will forgive you, despite the rotten things you have done in your past. There are no limits to the hurts He can heal you from, no matter what people have done to you. There are no limits to how much you can grow in your spiritual walk, no limits to His restoration for your life and no limits to how many new friends He can bring into your life. And there are definitely no limits to how happy you can be when you finally meet the right one, and no limits to how healthy, prosperous, happy, whole, youthful, and wonderful your life can be.

Best of all, there are no limits to His love for you and His desire to fulfill your longings. He can love you higher, deeper, longer, and more intimately than anyone you have ever known. Just come to Him as a child, tell Him you want a life without limits and that you believe He is over everything in the Earth and the universe. He knows no boundaries. Tell Him you will go as far with Him as He will let you go and you will commit to love Him without boundaries and believe Him without limits. He will be so pleased! Who knows what He will show you because of your belief?

Today, take some time to think about the way you pray to God. Are your prayers faith-filled, expressing hopes for the impossible? Or are you putting God in a little box and experiencing only the things that your wee little mind can imagine? Get out of that little box and start asking God for bigger things, believing He can make them happen.

Remember, He can resurrect something from the dead, He can restore something that was lost, and He can create something that never was before. He longs to show you His power and He especially longs to see you take your faith into daring directions which cause Him to exclaim, "Never have I seen such faith before!"

What eye has not seen and ear has not heard and has not entered into the heart of man, [all that] God has prepared [made and keeps ready] for those who love Him [who hold Him in affectionate reverence, promptly obeying Him and gratefully recognizing the benefits He has bestowed]. (1 Corinthians 2:9b, AMP)

A New Vision for a New Kind of Relationship

One of the greatest and most comforting truths is that when one door opens, another closes; but often we look so long and regretfully upon the closed door that we do not see the one that is open for us.

— ANONYMOUS

CHAPTER NINE

What's a Dysfunctional Relationship?

What exactly is a dysfunctional relationship? When I began asking God this question, He took me on an important journey of discovering the beauty of healthy relationships founded in Him. Not everyone has enjoyed a history of functional relationships or the example of loving parents to be our compass for a healthy union. We need one.

Song of Solomon is a good start. Everyone should read it and take note of how the two lovers lovingly upheld each other's honor and dignity. The more you fill your heart and mind with pictures of a beautiful, healthy relationship, the more an unhealthy relationship will become unattractive to you.

People-watching is one of my favorite pasttimes. I especially note people that relate well to each other and those that don't. Sometimes it breaks my heart to observe women making some of the same mistakes I made. I cringe when I see a woman belittling her husband in front of others. I ache inside when I hear someone call a man stupid, slow, or immature in front of his children. Likewise, I feel the familiar pain and humiliation that a woman feels when her husband tells her to "shut-up" loud enough for others to hear. It is so sad how we can treat the ones we claim to love. No wonder some people call their marriage a living hell.

The following is a list of the dysfunctional and functional characteristics of a relationship. I even tape lists to my refrigerator door, because I want my sons to learn what a healthy relationship is *before* they started dating. Take time to really study these characteristics and as you read the attributes of a healthy relationship, feel free to get excited about the fact that your Father in Heaven can provide just such a person for you!

Qualities of an Unhealthy Relationship

1. You sense that you are only truly accepted when you are behaving in a way that pleases your partner. You are always seeking their approval.

2. You feel unbalanced and confused and sometimes second-guess your personal intelligence and mental stability.

3. You feel like you have settled for less than God has for you.

4. You feel as though you are never good enough.

5. You feel confined and closed-in and your outside friendships have been diminished or discounted.

6. There are always issues to fix in the relationship.

7. Your needs are secondary and you feel as though you don't have a voice in decision-making discussions.

8. You see how others are respected by their partners and inwardly wish that you were respected the same way.

9. You don't really want to stay, but you are afraid to leave.

10. You feel you have to defend and justify your partner's behavior to friends and relatives.

11. You feel like you are on a roller coaster—sometimes experiencing thrilling highs and horrible lows.

12. Certain dynamics and situations in the relationship make you feel anxious and restless.

13. You still feel lonely frequently.

Characteristics of a Healthy Relationship

1. You feel respected and honored.

2. You can reveal your deepest feelings and secrets to that person with the utmost trust.

3. You feel more alive and joyful and find yourself smiling often.

4. Your partner is not insecure, and allows you to grow and better yourself through new challenges and the pursuit of your dreams.

5. You are equally yoked, spiritually, mentally, and socially, while you still maintain individual differences.

6. Each brings healing to the other through openness, stability, and security.

7. Each person in the relationship has allowed plenty of time and space from past relationships, and is positive about the future.

8. God has confirmed through family and friends that this person is a good fit for you.

9. You and your partner develop and maintain close friendships with others and neither of you is threatened by this.

10. Your partner is more than you would have known to ask for.

11. You feel fully accepted—whether you are being fun and silly or whether you are sick and just feeling "ugly."

12. When separated from each other, although you miss him or her, you do not feel alone.

13. You find yourself constantly thanking God for that person.

If you are like me, you read the first list and could identify with some of the characteristics of an unhealthy relationship. Most of us have experienced at least a few of the symptoms of being in a relationship that wasn't quite right. Perhaps we thought that the relationship was not out of the ordinary, or maybe, we even thought it was normal. After all, we tend to define *normal* by the environment in which we were raised, even though it may have been faulty.

The second list regarding a healthy relationship made a real impact on my vision for dating again. If you read the second list and found yourself longing for such a relationship, as I did, then I congratulate you. Your eyes have been opened and you can see that the promise of a healthy relationship is truly exciting. This kind of relationship is within your reach when you trust God to give you discernment and direction in your dating life. The Bible says that the steps of a righteous man are ordered by the Lord and I have found many times that God has directed me away from potentially harmful situations. He has our best interests at heart—always.

Take one more look at the second list. This time, instead of viewing this list with a potential mate in mind, view the list with someone else in mind. Jesus. Then take a few minutes to thank Him for being who He is—the perfect lover of your soul.

Love endures long and is patient and kind;. love never is envious nor boils over with jealousy, it is not boastful or vainglorious, does not display itself haughtily. It is not conceited (arrogant and inflated with pride); it is not rude (unmannerly) and does not act unbecomingly. Love (God's love in us) does not insist on its own rights or its own way, for it is not self-seeking; it is not touchy or fretful or resentful; it takes no account of the evil done to it (it pays no attention to a suffered wrong). It does not rejoice at injustice and unrighteousness, but rejoices when right and truth prevail.

Love bears up under anything and everything that comes, is ever ready to believe the best of every person, its hopes are fadeless under all circumstances, and it endures everything (without weakening).

Love never fails (never fades out or becomes obsolete or comes to an end).... And so faith, hope, love abide, these three; but the greatest of these is love. (1 Corinthians 13:4-8a,13, AMP)

CHAPTER TEN

Attraction Isn't the Only Thing

We have all dated someone in the past, which at the time, we thought was the love of our life, only to look back now and say, "What was I thinking?" It is easy to laugh about some of the mistakes we made earlier in our lives, when our hormones were raging and we didn't know any better, but how do we know we won't make those same mistakes again?

Attraction is very powerful. Infatuation is even more powerful. Although it doesn't last forever, it can draw unsuspecting people down the wrong path in the beginning months of a dating relationship. Our society tells us to be led strictly by our feelings. Hollywood makes movies that are misleading and fictionalized, yet the American public longs to have the exact same thing happen in their own lives. You meet someone and the attraction is so strong that you just cannot fight it. A week later, you have moved in together and live happily ever after. And what is really sad is our society's almost dreamlike, romantic notion that it doesn't even matter if you are already married when you meet that other person. If you can't fight those feelings, you just have to give in to them.

If simple attraction were the standard by which you measured whether or not you should be with someone, you would be with hundreds of people. There are many attractive people out there and even after you are married, you will still be occasionally attracted to someone. Does that mean that every time it happens you should act on it? Let's face it; you just cannot trust your feelings and emotions. If you acted on every single one, you would be a mess.

That means there has to be a different tool in place to examine whether someone is right for you or not. Simple attraction is going to have to be moved way down your list of qualities to look for in someone. It is important, no doubt, and fun. Attraction is like the big picture window in a tour bus that allows you to take in the beautiful scenery, but if it becomes the bus driver, you've got problems.

Below is a list of qualities of which you should be aware. There are many ways to determine if someone is going to be a good person to date, and a likely candidate for marriage. You have heard it before, but I'll say it again. Don't *ever* date someone that you could not marry, it's just the ABC's of dating. The first list contains negative *red lights* that you should be wary of. The second list contains positive *green lights* that signify you are on the right track.

Red Lights

• *Bad Reputation:* The public's perception of this person is very important. If you hear that someone is a womanizer, can't keep a job, does drugs, or has any other issues, stay away. If you choose to ignore this first very important red flag, you are not exhibiting sound wisdom and proceed at your own risk. A reputation is like the label on a can—it tells you what you're getting.

• *Quick Attachment* (instant neediness): Mature, healthy people want to take their time to get to know you and build a friendship with you. If someone floods you with attention immediately after the first date and is already stating that you could be the one, don't be flattered—be wary. These people are usually flighty and lacking stability. They like the rush of a fast moving, intense relationship and usually have immature expectations and short-lived commitments.

• *Belittles Your Opinions:* If your opinions or feelings on a subject are shot down, argued with, dismissed, or made fun of, you are in trouble. This kind of person has control issues and usually feels the need to dominate. You do not need someone second-guessing you and causing self-doubt. Stay true to everything you believe in. If that person doesn't feel the same, and cannot at the very least respectfully disagree—big red flag—they are not for you.

• *Not Equally Yoked Spiritually:* This is a hard one. Most people feel that if someone goes to the same church or just goes to church at all, they must be a good person to date. Watch out if that's your perception. You must be well matched spiritually to make a relationship work. Wars have been fought over religious differences and for good reason—it is a very emotional issue. Make sure the person you date is as spiritually mature as you are and has had some time to work out his or her own faith.

• *The Blamer:* These people blame everyone else for all their misfortunes and seem to have a hard luck story for everything. Their ex was crazy, their boss is an egomaniac, the cops have it in for them, their co-workers are jealous, their parents don't love them, etc. Before long, he or she will be blaming you for everything that goes wrong. Watch how this person deals with conflict in his life. If he is not a humble person who knows how to take personal responsibility for his behavior, you'd better head in the opposite direction.

• *The Flirt:* I don't care how society laughs it off, flirting is never harmless. Never! It is totally inappropriate and has no place in a sincere committed relationship. It is only a sign that the flirt has some serious insecurity issues and needs constant reassurance from the opposite sex.

• *Anger Issues:* In the road rage society we live in today, there is simply no tolerance for inconvenience anymore. People who freely give themselves over to anger usually are not considerate of those they vent on. Their anger takes over and becomes more important than the precious people around them. These people often leave broken and bleeding people in their wake. If you are on a date with someone and his or her behavior makes you feel uncomfortable, uneasy, or frightened, get away quickly. Don't ever try to reason it away by making excuses that they may just be having a bad day. One episode is enough to give you the big picture.

Green Lights

• *Good Reputation:* Make sure that you consistently hear positive feedback on the behavior and attitudes of this person. The people that give those recommendations should be those whose opinions you value. "A good name is more desirable than great riches." If you marry someone with a good reputation, you enter into his or her blessing.

• *Kindness and Courtesy:* Watch how he or she treats the people that serve you. If they are respectful, patient, kind, and generous, you will learn their basic attitude toward people. If they don't complain or criticize others, it is a good indication that you won't ever be in the line of fire either. This also includes watching how they drive. If someone cuts them off and your date graciously lets it go, you have found a good, balanced person without anger issues.

• *People Lovers:* They love people. They don't say things like, "People get on my nerves," or "He's an idiot." They defend people and are helpful and patient with others. They don't gossip and they always look for the best in someone. It's not that they are naive or turn a blind eye to wrongdoing—they just accept people where they are. These kind of people remind me most of Jesus.

• *God Seekers:* They seek God for all the major decisions in life. This is what I love about King David. He always made sure he was in the will of God and it made him the greatest King of Israel. You want someone who has the Bible as the moral compass for his life. When you marry someone like that, you won't be taken on a wild ride of risks and failures. You will learn together when God opens and closes a door, and you will honor God with your decisions.

• *Financially Responsible:* This goes for both men and women. I have met so many women that want to marry someone who will fix their financial mess. Both people should bring some assets into a marriage. Both people should have a healthy attitude toward finances and both should agree on tithing as the number one priority of their finances.

• *Honoring of Parents:* These people honor their fathers and mothers. This doesn't mean that they agree with everything their parents say, it just means that they show them respect and honor and have a healthy attitude toward the authority figures in their life. Why is this so important? Where do you think your children will learn how to treat you when you are older? It will be from the way you and your spouse treat your parents.

• *Walking in the Fruit of the Spirit:* "You will know them by their fruits" (Matthew 7:16, ASB). The Bible has supplied you with the best list to look for in a date—the fruit of the Holy Spirit. They are love, joy, peace, patience, kindness, goodness, faithfulness, gentleness, and self-control. If you are seeing fruit opposite from this, strife, meanness, unfaithfulness, or extreme impatience, you are dealing with either an immature Christian or someone who may not be a Christian at all.

It is time for you to get choosy and lay down the law about the kind of person you will allow into your life. This may include deflecting unwanted attention and attraction from the other sex. It is not that these people are being improper or intrusive; you just don't want to lead them on, and it's a very good practice to get in the habit of addressing the opposite sex properly. When you are married this will be second nature to you, and will prepare you for the traps that can befall a marriage.

Most attractions start with the eye. That first eye contact is huge. It's funny how you can see someone across the room, make eye contact, and have a connection with them. There is a powerful exchange between two people during even a second of intense eye contact. People are good at giving off vibes, and most of them are sent with the eyes. If you sense someone giving you the *eye* and they are not the kind of person you should be dating, don't be a victim; politely look away and don't look back. Then, ask Jesus to loose you from that attraction.

Don't misunderstand; attraction is not evil, and I am praying that I will be *tremendously* attracted to my mate. Attraction serves a great purpose in a relationship and is a lot of fun, too. The whole purpose of this chapter is to give you the wisdom to know when your attraction to someone is overruling your discernment. It is to make you aware that the power of extreme and unquestioned attraction can sometimes be a counterfeit feeling of a *genuine* affection for someone. As you pray and progress slowly into a relationship, God will give you a peace when you're on the right track with someone.

CHAPTER ELEVEN

Taking Responsibility for Your Relationship

Shortly after my divorce, I attended a relationship workshop based on the Book of Song of Solomon. The speaker was especially gifted at bringing Scripture to life and giving the audience a wonderful understanding of God's creative and exciting design for marriage. I was already thinking that I would meet my prince any day and needed to be able to spot a worthy candidate. I figured the workshop would teach me what to look for in a man. It did, and then some.

For the two days of the workshop, we studied Scripture and did a lot of laughing and crying as the speaker expounded truth after truth. A friend of mine who had recently separated from her husband, decided to attend the workshop with him as a last effort to repair their marriage. As I sat by them, I noticed they were holding hands and opening up to each other. The Scripture was softening their hearts and they were reconnecting. I could see tears in their eyes as spiritual truths were opening their eyes. I remember thinking, "If only my ex-husband could have attended a workshop like this, maybe it could have *fixed* him."

Almost everything I learned at the workshop supported the notion that I had married a loser. As the speaker read from the Song of Solomon and explained how the king spoke softly and tenderly toward his new wife, it only sadly reminded me that my ex-husband had rarely spoken to me in that way. No wonder our relationship was doomed.

When we married, we hardly knew each other—only a short five months, it was the proverbial shotgun wedding. I would not recommend it to anyone, but we did what seemed right and brought three extraordinary boys into the world. Our boys are wonderful, healthy, talented, and handsome, too! I wouldn't change anything. I just wish I could have changed my husband. He was definitely the problem. If only *he* would have acted right. Right?

The second night of the program, the discussion was getting more serious. The speaker was discussing marriage and gave us a list of sixteen things that you should never do to your spouse. These behaviors would tear down the foundation of a marriage. I ripped my purse open to get a pen and paper. I knew I was about to see a list of the things that my husband had done to me and I wanted to note them so I could make sure I did not date the same kind of guy.

He began, "You should *never* ... raise your voice at your mate."

I had a private conversation going in my head that said, *Yes, he always yelled at me.*

The list continued, "You should never publicly embarrass your mate."

Oh, my husband did that to me all the time! My case against my ex was growing and I was being exonerated.

The list continued again:

- You should never call each other names.
- You should never have conflict in front of your children.
- You should never talk of your conflicts outside of the home.
- You should never use sex to punish each other.
- You should never touch in anger.
- You should never bring up things from the past.
- You should never stomp out of your home in anger.
- You should never freeze the other person out.
- You should never bring up the in-laws.
- You should never try to reason in the face of pain, because pain cancels out reason.
- You should never let the sun go down on your anger.
- You should never reverse the argument to "Remember when?"
- You should never interrupt while your spouse is talking.
- You should never harden yourself against your mate.

I mentally checked off all the things on the list that my husband had put me through, and my anger was burning. Now I had proof that he was a monster. While I was sitting in my smug, "holier than thou," Phariseeism, the Holy

Spirit sweetly suggested something to me. "Why don't you go back through that list and mark off the things that *you* did in your marriage?"

Ouch, that hurt! That certainly wasn't *my* idea. I would have never thought of that on my own. Who willingly sits down to take an inventory of all the mistakes and hurt you may have inflicted on someone else? That is not even natural. However, we do not have a natural God.

I slowly looked at the list and picked up my pen. I had to check off the first one. Yes, I did that. Then, the second ... I did that too. I checked the third and fourth and so on down the list. I still have the list and almost all of the "You should never's" are checked.

I sat in stunned silence. The blinders were gone, three fingers were pointing back at me, and my glass house was shattering. The rest of the service was drawing to a close around me while I was mentally in my own world. I had no excuses. I had retaliated and sometimes instigated all the things mentioned on the list. Genuine remorse welled up in my heart as I began to grieve that I had done such things to my ex. I had to tell my ex-husband that I was sorry. He would think I was crazy, I knew that, but I could not rest until I had made it right.

I don't know if he remembers the phone call, but I certainly do. I apologized through tears for all the ways that I contributed to the breakdown of our marriage and I especially expressed my remorse for any pain I had ever caused him. I'm sure my humility took him quite by surprise and he could have taken advantage of the moment by agreeing and demanding justice, but he didn't. It was obvious that the Holy Spirit was monitoring our conversation. He had started this whole thing, and He would see that it finished to the glory of God.

My ex-husband kindly replied that we *both* made mistakes, but all mistakes were forgiven and we could be friends. Of course, we could. That had been God's idea from the very beginning: for me to come to a place where I would give forgiveness and receive forgiveness. It was not God's intention for me to see my mistakes and then wallow in guilt for the rest of my life. The only reason God lets us see our mistakes is so that we can make them right with His help and then grow in wisdom from those mistakes. Now, the enemy would like to take those mistakes and beat us up with them, but since I immediately made it right, he had no ammunition against me. It's hard to beat someone up with mistakes that are forgiven and gone.

Taking responsibility for my share of mistakes in my failed marriage was huge for me. We cannot move forward spiritually with even a hint of Phariseeism or pride in our hearts. We *all* make mistakes and no one is perfect. A great relationship takes two people actively seeking to put the interests of the other ahead of their own. We must realize the important part we ourselves play in whether a relationship is a success or a failure.

Don't worry, I am not going to ask you to sit and list all your mistakes. However, I *am* going to ask you to review the above list very carefully. I doubt that there are many people who could go through that whole list without checking off at least one item that they have done. I can attest wholeheartedly that some of those very actions were what unraveled my own marriage. In fact, our marriage was off to a bad start because even in our dating and engagement periods, we were breaking rules on the list. But, now I have been educated and I can make sure that future relationships don't involve the same actions. So can you.

We can ask God to remove these habits from our lives and we can practice listening to, and disagreeing with, others within the proper boundaries. Keep reviewing the list for the next few days so that it becomes part of your thinking. If you have been like me, and need to ask for forgiveness from someone, go with God's blessing.

P.S. My friend who attended the workshop with her estranged husband has had her marriage completely restored. They moved back in together shortly after the conference and are still happily serving the Lord together today.

CHAPTER TWELVE

The Sleeping Giant

Long ago in a land far away, there once lived a girl name Mayla. Mayla lived in a small village in a time and place where many fanciful creatures also lived. Although for the most part, her village was safe, there was an occasional threat from giants in the land. The giants were as big as the tallest trees in the forest and very mighty. They could be a bit on the grumpy side and the villagers were terrified of them. Fortunately, the giants did not come around her village unless they were disturbed or incited in some way.

Mayla was seventeen, the oldest of four siblings, and was becoming a beautiful young woman. Her father was a lumberjack and her mother a seamstress. Every day, Mayla and her siblings walked to the cottage school where they were students. Since the village was so small, there were only eight other teens that were close to her age. One of them, Hanson, was eighteen and the oldest. He was a man in every way and he had eyes only for Mayla.

One day, the schoolmaster informed the class that they were to take a field trip. They would be traveling to a nearby village to join another class of students their age.

They were instructed to follow the road through the woods, stay close together, and by all means, keep their voices low so as not to attract any giants. Although Mayla listened to the instructions, she was rarely frightened by the thought of giants. She felt confident that nothing could ever happen to her. After all, she was a teenager, and teenagers were invincible.

As the small group started their journey, Mayla and Hanson fell to the rear so that they could talk as they walked. Hanson was quite charming and there had been a budding romance between them within the last year. He had deep blue eyes and a wide smile with dimples. Although she had known him since they were small children, her girlhood crush had increased into stronger feelings and her innocent fondness for him had developed into full-blown fantasies when she thought about him.

As they walked behind the group, his hand reached out to take hers. As soon as he touched her, she could feel sensations of excitement. They had held hands many times before, but it seemed that lately she wanted to press further. Although they had never spoken of it, Hanson was thinking the same thing.

She felt a tug on her arm that gently pulled her off the trail. She looked at Hanson with curious eyes. He answered with a wink as they quietly left the rest of the group and hid behind a tree, unnoticed. The rest of the group walked on, chatting away.

Mayla knew that they were placing themselves in danger by separating from the group, but she didn't care. Her desires were too strong, the opportunity was perfect, and he was absolutely awesome. Anyway, there probably wasn't a giant around for miles.

They began to kiss and found a soft spot in the grass so that they could lie down and make out for a while. As they kissed more aggressively, Mayla paused a moment and lifted her head. She heard a faint sound in the woods. It sounded like footsteps getting closer. At first, she reasoned that it was a large animal, but soon it became obvious that it was much bigger than an animal. The steps grew heavier and she could hear tree limbs cracking and breaking with force. The ground began to shake as if a small earthquake was being unleashed. Mayla sat up as a dread began to engulf her. She knew what was coming their way. It was a giant.

Hanson did not waste a second and jumped up to run away. As he ran, he called out to her to follow, but she couldn't move. Her legs were frozen. The giant was only a few yards away and she could see his eyes. He looked straight at her and she felt like a small animal trapped by a hungry lion. She could not scream and she only felt lifeless and limp as she simply allowed him to approach her. She slowly closed her eyes as she anticipated that he would crush her with one quick blow.

She felt herself being lifted into the air and kept her eyes shut, afraid to see what would happen next. The giant started walking as he carried her in his arms. Apparently, he wasn't going to kill her just yet. Maybe he would toy with her awhile and then put her out of her misery. As he carried her, they traveled down a path for a few minutes until she finally mustered up enough courage to open her eyes. She could see that they were approaching a large, giant house. It must be his house.

Soon after, they came to the house and the giant carried her in. The door slammed shut and she was thrust into an enclosure on a table that resembled a birdcage. She was alone, imprisoned, and there was no one to help her. The giant walked away and she slumped down in the cage, too afraid to move.

She was so mad at herself. Why did she let her guard down! She had just made one small mistake and now she had been carried away to be held captive by an uncaring giant who was probably going to destroy her. Why did she have to leave the safety of the group? Why did she let Hanson's big blue eyes turn her into a blubbering fool who threw caution to the wind? What was she going to do?

As she considered her plight, the giant began rustling around in the kitchen, apparently making preparations for a meal. She wondered if *she* would be the main course. He didn't seem to acknowledge her in any way except to look at the cage periodically to make sure she was staying put. He seemed impersonal and uncaring as he went about his business in the huge kitchen. Maybe he just wanted to keep her as a toy or a pet. He *must* have used the cage for others. Whatever happened to them?

She began to examine her surroundings and was surprised to see that there was a latch on the cage and it could easily be opened, even by someone as small as she was. She felt a surge of hope. If somehow she could escape while the giant wasn't looking, she could jump from the table to the chair below and onto the floor. The crack under the door was large enough that she could slide underneath it and be on her way to freedom. It was worth a try. Anything was better than perishing at the hands of the giant, but what should she do? He kept eyeing the cage. How would she have a moment to escape?

Suddenly there was a huge crash in the kitchen. She turned to see the giant who was enraged as he began to bang an empty container against the wall. He threw cabinet doors open and growled as his hands swept across empty cupboards. Whatever it was that he was looking for was evidently missing. He went on for several minutes, throwing a tantrum and grunting in enormous frustration. His grunts turned to low moans and then he sat down in a chair, all his energy drained. He glared at the cage and then looked at the wall in front of him. He laid his head against the wall behind him. It appeared that he was going to take a nap.

That was it! She would wait for him to fall asleep, then sneak out of the cage, and be on her way to freedom. He was looking at the cage as his eyes began to droop. Every once in awhile a noise would rouse him and he would grunt and jerk, but he was slowly getting sleepier. She decided to help the giant fall asleep, and like a small caged bird, she began humming and singing in low beautiful tones. The entrancing sounds soothed the giant, until his heavy breathing became a low snore. He was out.

Mayla slowly lifted the latch to the cage, slipped out, and tiptoed to the end of the table. As she took a leap to the chair below, there was a small creaking noise when her foot hit the seat. Paralyzed, she didn't move, and looked quickly at the giant. He briefly stopped snoring, jerked, and then returned back to his slumber. She wasted no time in jumping to the floor. As soon as she was on the ground, she moved quickly toward the door, lay down, and slid under it to safety on the other side. When she was outside of the house, she ran like she had never run before in her entire life. She ran all the way home.

As she approached her village, the people saw her and the whole village erupted in excitement that she was safe and had returned home. They all gathered around her, crying and hugging her. No one scolded her, but they didn't need to. She already knew in her heart that she would never allow herself to be caught by another giant. Hanson slowly approached her to tell her he was sorry. With her eyes full of tears, she hugged him, and assured him that from now on, they would abide by the rules. Everyone agreed and the village celebrated for the rest of the day.

So what is the moral of this little tale? You are a single adult and there is a giant raging inside you. It's called sexual desire. Whenever you find yourself in a compromising situation, such as alone in a secluded place with the opposite sex, about to engage in innocent, stolen kisses (or more), the giant within you is aroused and comes to carry you away. Before you know it, you have become captive to the giant and held prisoner by your own desires. It seems that there is no way that you can control them anymore, and it happens over and over again. It is not about people anymore, it's about you and your giant. The giant does not care about you; it only wants to own you and keep you imprisoned. The giant is unbelievably strong and he is not your friend, just your captor. As long as the giant is awake, he keeps you bound and captive. The only way that you can escape is to put the giant to sleep. Once he is asleep, you are no longer under his control.

So, how do you put your sexual desires to sleep until the time comes when they can be awakened and you are married? Don't feed them. You cannot stimulate, or even humor them, in any way. You must let them lie completely dormant because disturbing them can arouse them and prevent you from becoming free.

These desires become aroused by many things. Sexually charged television shows, movies, romance novels, alcohol, flirting, pornography, inappropriate joking about sex, suggestive music, hormones, revealing clothing, phone sex—and the list goes on.

You have to be proactive in keeping the giant asleep. In doing this, you are protecting yourself, and even others, from something that can be harmful to you and your wholeness as a single person. Sex within a marriage is wonderful and totally fulfilling, but sex before marriage is a giant that will take you captive, keeping you from the real pleasure God wants to show you with His blessing. Just as Mayla softly sang sweet melodies to put the giant asleep, your voice must do the same for you.

You must keep your conversation positive and wholesome as you encourage yourself. Saying things like, "I just can't help it; I have needs," is counterproductive to putting the giant asleep. You must say things like, "I can do all things through Christ and that includes keeping myself pure." It is sweet music to you and your Lord.

Secondly, you must learn to control your thought life. You cannot allow yourself to fantasize about someone for even a second. The second you allow fantasy to take over, you have changed from the driver's seat to the back seat and your mind is a maniacal driver.

If you are attracted to your boss and are tempted to fantasize about him, *don't*. Not your boss, or your professor, or your preacher, or your neighbor, or another parent on your child's soccer team, or your best friend's spouse. Not even Hollywood actors or athletes, comedians or political figures. *No one.* Do not fantasize about *anyone.* Not even someone you just started dating. Fantasizing will take you into zones that can ruin a relationship. It may seem harmless in the beginning but it is powerful and feeds desires inside of you that know no boundaries.

I know this is a challenge and probably sounds crazy in today's society, but don't do it. Someday, when you are married, you will be able to stay true to your spouse even in your thought life.

That's the goal of what we are doing. We are preparing you for a successful relationship and a great marriage that will survive the statistics.

I am sure this chapter has opened up *a can of worms* for some of you. Some of the things we discussed may not appear important to you and some of them may be new and uncomfortable. Just ask God how He wants you to conduct your dating life and believe me, if you ask, He will answer. If He asks you to change a few habits, just be willing. Remember, He is a concerned parent and He only wants the best for you. He wants to give you someone better than you can imagine right now. He's the one that raises the bar for us when we are content to keep it low. Let God treat you like the precious gift that you are. Let Him give you a dating relationship fit for a prince or princess, because that's what you are!

As you get a new vision for the kind of dating life you want to engage in, you have to be completely aware of the pitfalls and traps that can destroy you or your relationship.

When the day comes that God gives you that special person in marriage, sex will be something beautiful, special, and purposeful that unites you and your spouse. Something that is no longer caged, but free ... like a bird.

Practicing to Be a Good Mate

～

Striving for success without hard work is like trying to

harvest where you haven't planted.

– DAVID BLY

CHAPTER THIRTEEN

For Richer or Poorer

I have heard it said that there are no dress rehearsals in life. Well, I beg to differ on this one subject. Now, before you get married, is a great time to practice healthy behavior in all the areas of your life. This is the time to reclaim your mind, your thought life, and rehearse how a healthy person acts in a relationship. And who will be the person who you will be practicing with? God.

When you learn to treat God with true love, faithfulness, and respect, you will find that same reverence leaking into your actions toward those around you. When you learn to be committed to Him on the good *and* the bad days, you will learn to stay committed to others during the good *and* the bad times. When you learn to stay faithful to God, even when you sometimes doubt, you will learn to stay faithful to your future spouse even when doubt is looming.

Speaking of commitment, let's consider the vows that one takes when making the biggest commitment in life—marriage:

I promise to:

Love, comfort, honor and keep you

For better or worse,

For richer or poorer,

In sickness and in health,

Forsaking all others,

And be faithful only to you

As long as we both shall live.

We have all heard them, but have we practiced them? It seems that when I said them to my ex-husband, I was hardly aware of the true covenant that they represented. It was just part of the wedding ceremony, which was partly a blur because of wedding jitters and nerves. I know I did not always honor him, and when the worse part of "for better or worse" came around, I was not prepared for it.

Recently, as I was taking my evening walk, I began praying to the Lord, telling Him how I was grieved that I had not lived those vows better in my marriage. I truly wanted to be a good, no, a *great* vow keeper. He told me He would teach me.

How would He do that? Vow Training 101? Sounded interesting. I voiced the vows out loud and told God I wanted to practice keeping my vows with Him. It was a happy thought as I finished my walk home and I had all the good intentions in the world of remembering those vows.

A few days passed and I was doing great, but then my vows were tested. I had been laid off from a job several months earlier and was squeaking by on weekly unemployment checks. I barely had enough for the essentials and was believing by faith that God would provide and keep me from any financial crises. Unpredictably, there was a glitch in the system and my weekly check was not deposited. Bills were due and I found myself in despair over the mistake. My first thought was, "God, how could You let this happen? Are You even there?"

We have all been there. Something doesn't turn out the way we thought and we find ourselves wondering where God is in this whole thing. Or maybe, someone cancels an outing with us and we spend the evening alone wondering if God cares about us anymore.

While I was busy doubting God, I heard a small reminder in my heart, "for richer or poorer." Tears welled up in my eyes and I said out loud, "Yes Lord, for richer or poorer for as long as I live." I realized my mistake. I have always only wanted to love and believe God in the good times. Sometimes in the bad times, I have disconnected, retreated, doubted, and run away. God was teaching me that in the bad times, we still stand by those we love and we do not vent our frustrations on them.

We live in a fallen world. The Word says that we will have tribulations. Employers will lay us off, loved ones will get cancer, businesses will go bankrupt, and yes, people will disappoint us. When these things happen, will I stay faithful to the one true God? Or will I challenge His very existence? Will you?

What about family and friends? When worse comes along, do we write them off? Uncle Joe, who's in prison, the sister that grates on your nerves, or the boss that has an ego as big as Texas? Can we still love and honor them as long as they are in our lives? It takes practice and lots of prayer.

Another part of those vows is, "In sickness and in health." I have known people that have stuck with their spouses through years and years of sickness and tragedy. On the other hand, I have also known those that have left their sick or dying spouse to die alone because the challenge was too great and they did not have the fortitude (or the character) to stay. It's a very sensitive subject, but maybe it's one that we should spend some time thinking about. What is your commitment level to the person you are going to marry? A good predictor of that answer will be your commitment level to God and others right now.

My best friend, Kim, is the most faithful person I have ever met. She married a man twenty-five years ago with two daughters from a previous marriage that have a rare genetic condition. Both daughters, Emily and Callie, are severely disabled and have the functions of a six-week-old baby. Although they are full grown, they are both about the size of a four-year-old child. They have to be fed, changed, bathed, treated with breathing apparatus, and require twenty-four-hour care. Every other weekend Kim and her husband have the girls, and every one of those visits requires that they must stay home the entire weekend to care for the girls. They have missed many, many activities because they cannot leave their home when Emily and Callie are there. It is hard work, and most of that burden falls on Kim.

Their situation is further complicated because Kim and her husband now have their own two healthy daughters. Sometimes they cannot be at the girls' school or church activities because they are home caring for Emily and Callie.

I have seen my dear friend cry many times because her life with her two healthy girls is limited on those weekends. I've also seen her frustrated with regurgitated food all over her, faithfully staying up during the night to make sure someone was breathing right and spending endless hours home alone while the rest of the family went to church and other functions. I've seen the sacrifices she has made, and it has affected me deeply.

Emily and Callie were only expected to live to about nine years of age, but they are now over thirty (most likely due to the thorough care they receive). Kim is still caring for them, so she has been doing this for the *entire* twenty-five years of their marriage. Did she get more than she bargained for? You bet! But she loves her husband, and she has a faithful spirit about her.

I fully expect to get to Heaven and see her get a "special saint" reward that will make it worth it all for her and I will be the loudest one in the crowd screaming and whistling for her. Not only that, I expect that Emily and Callie (fully healed in Heaven) will have many thanks for Kim's love and faithfulness.

In the meantime, I have learned what faithfulness really is as I have seen it modeled in my best friend. She's faithful in all her ways and it's all because she is first faithful to Christ. Kim has been faithful to Him in the "better or worse" times in her life and it has manifested in her relationship with others.

Today, meditate on the wedding vows and what they mean. Ask God to make these vows a way of life for you in the way you treat Him and everyone around you. Perhaps you need to take some time to evaluate yourself as to whether you could really be faithful in all the areas of a marriage. For better or worse, for richer or poorer, in sickness and in health, and forsaking all others as long as you both shall live. Be honest in the areas that you have doubts, ask God to strengthen you in those areas and then thank Him that change is on the way.

CHAPTER FOURTEEN

Slicing and Dicing

Our whole society has become careless and harsh in the way we converse with each other. Men don't watch their language in front of women and children anymore, argumentative terms like "talk to the hand" permeate our society, and sarcasm is rampant.

Just think of your favorite programs on television. My sons and I sometimes watch a popular television show that is a perfect example of this. It's a sitcom that features a husband and wife who seem to love each other, but constantly berate, antagonize, and use sarcasm to make the other appear stupid. It may seem harmless, but what is it teaching us?

I have seen sports talk shows dripping with sarcastic, witty comebacks, reality TV shows where cutting sarcasm is the primary language and even political debates where candidates show their cleverness by their ability to show the inferiority of their opposition and predecessors with cynical remarks. It may only be television, but if you are not careful, you will become desensitized to it and it will become the way you communicate with your family, friends, and even your dates. When this happens, the eventual outcome will be that someone will get hurt.

I looked up the definition of *sarcasm* and was really taken aback by what the underlying meaning is.

Merriam Webster defines sarcasm as: *To tear flesh, bite the lips in rage; sneer. 1) A sharp and often satirical or ironic utterance designed to cut or give pain. 2) A mode of satirical wit depending for its effect on bitter, caustic, and often ironic language that is usually directed against an individual.*

Wikipedia defines it: *"Mockery; sarcasm is sneering, jesting, or mocking at a person, situation, or thing. It is a type of verbal irony intended to insult or wound. It is sometimes viewed as an expression of concealed anger, annoyance, and/ or ignorance."*

As you can easily deduct, sarcasm has no place in a healthy, respectful relationship. You need to start eliminating it from your communication now. Even when you are referring to your ex or those who have hurt you, do not use it. Why? Sarcasm can easily turn into trash talk and then you have really crossed into a dangerous zone. Not for your target, but for *you*. It causes you to gradually start dehumanizing people with a progressive lack of concern for their feelings.

To *dehumanize* is when one asserts the inferiority of another through subtle or overt acts or statements. It is to remove or deny the human qualities, characteristics, or attributes of a person to make both their pain and their individuality irrelevant—like calling someone a dog, ass, or other derogatory terms.

Dehumanization was actually a tactic used by the Germans during the Holocaust to make it easier for them to kill the Jews without feeling guilt. As the Nazis called them names and reduced their value to that of animals, killing them was no more callous than killing stray dogs. Now I am not suggesting that you are on the road to starting a new Holocaust, but if you indulge in extreme sarcasm and dehumanizing behavior, it can turn *you* into an unfeeling person who does not care about hurting someone or their character. God does not want that for you. He wants you to stay fresh, kind, and courteous all the time so He can send you someone that you will treat respectfully.

Paul told us in Ephesians 4:29, NIV: *"Do not let any unwholesome talk come out of your mouths, but only what is helpful for building others up ... "* I will admit, that may be hard sometimes. There have been occasions when a negative conversation about someone was starting around me, and although inwardly I agreed with the opinions being expressed, I had to say something nice like, "Well, she's getting better all the time."

I do not want to allow my mind to judge or my mouth to say something derogatory about another human being, especially one of God's little lambs. Have I failed in this area? Many, many, times. We all have. Nevertheless, I can truthfully say that God impresses on me more every day how this is a roadblock in our spiritual journey and I have every desire to totally eliminate it.

I want my talk to be pure, uplifting, and faith-filled. My kids realized a long time ago that I don't play along with their jokes on one another. There have been times that they have begged me to pretend, or go along with a prank that they are playing, only to say, "Come on, Mom, you never play along."

That's right, I want my sons to have at least one person in their lives that they know will always be honest with them. They won't ever have to guess if I am deceiving them or hiding something from them. This is how our Heavenly Father parents us—you don't ever have to guess what He is doing or what the punch line is with Him. As one of my friends says, "God's not a tricker." He will always be straightforward, honest, and respectful to you.

Why is this so important to you now? Because you *never* want to initiate a type of communication in a dating relationship, or marriage, that can open the door for more hostile communication later. Sarcasm is a doorway. The negative way you talk about others is a doorway. Your attitude about how you respect, or disrespect people, is a doorway. It all reflects how you will eventually treat your mate. James 3:5-7, NIV says it this way when speaking about the tongue:

> ... *the tongue is a small part of the body, but it makes great boasts. Consider what a great forest is set on fire by a small spark. The tongue also is a fire, a world of evil among the parts of the body. It corrupts the whole person, sets the whole course of his life on fire, and is itself set on fire by hell.*

You never want to initiate a type of communication in a dating relationship or marriage that can open the doors for more hostile communication later. Sarcasm is such a spark. It opens the door to get more personal with your jabs and finally turns into insults and your weapon to win arguments. It's a fire you do not want to tamper with and it can destroy a relationship. Why would God use a forest fire as an example? Have you seen a forest after a fire has ravaged it? It is just a heap of ashes, death, and sadness. He is saying that it is a picture of the devastation left behind after you have used your tongue as a weapon against someone.

I am sure no one begins dating someone thinking that they are going to hurt that person with their words; it doesn't happen that way. It creeps in slowly, starting with just a small spark or a tiny remark. It also surfaces during a short moment of anger on a bad day when you are feeling a little grumpy. Then, suddenly, your green garden of a relationship has a small area of burned timber on it. Another remark, and another burn, and then another, and before long, there are unsightly burns all over your once beautiful garden. No one wants to stay in a garden that has been burned up. They will eventually seek greener pastures.

You may have some real questions right now. Here was my biggest question when God presented this to me: "Will I just be dull and no fun now? Can't I still joke around a little?" Of course you can; God has a sense of humor. Humor is a wonderful thing, but never at another's expense. You will have to pray and ask God to help you with this. It may be that you will make a few blunders and feel badly about them afterwards. That's okay; God uses your blunders to teach you. The very fact that you will feel badly about making a sarcastic remark or saying something derogatory about someone is a good sign that you are becoming more sensitive to what you are saying to others.

This may be one of those chapters that you are tempted to brush off and feel that it doesn't really pertain to you, but I encourage you to carefully evaluate whether your conversations about people are uplifting or negative. This is something that will leak into your married life and turn it sour in a very short time if you are not conscientious about the tone and motives behind your speech.

There is something beautiful about a couple that have been married for years and still speak to each other with courtesy and care. As you become aware of this now, as a single person, you can make the necessary changes and be one of those beautiful couples in the future. Just remember this and you will never go wrong, "If you can't say something nice, don't say anything at all."

CHAPTER FIFTEEN

Loneliness—Let It Serve a Purpose in Your Life

I used to have a real problem with cloudy days. I am just one of those people who needs her sunshine. For a while, it was a real thorn in my life. In the spring and summer, I was always happy and cheerful, almost giddy, and when fall came around, I could still cope because it is so beautiful where I live. Plus, I love football games and it just wouldn't be right in any other season. Even the Christmas season still distracted me from the weather with all the excitement of the holidays. But when January hit, ugh! Weeks of dreary, gray skies could send me into mild streaks of depression. If the sun poked its head out for just a day, it would revive me enough be hopeful again, but when the clouds returned, I was back to my grumpy self.

The Lord finally had to have a sit-down with me. When you don't have millions of dollars to run to a sunny paradise for the winter, you have to learn to have a new attitude about winter. It was clear to me that God was not going to change the seasons for me. Genesis 8:22, NIV verified that: *"As long as the earth endures, seedtime and harvest, cold and heat, summer and winter, day and night will never cease."*

When I found that Scripture, God spoke to my heart saying He was giving us a glimpse into the system that He set up for this Earth: seedtime and harvest, cold and heat, summer and winter, day and night. One will *always* follow the other. You will never have a harvest without sowing seed first, and you will never have summer without first going through a winter. But summer always comes back around. It's a promise!

These seasons are supposed to support one another in their purposes and one is the springboard for the other. How can you experience the beauty of dawn without first going through a few hours of night? How can you watch a beautiful sunset without knowing that a day is coming to close?

As Ecclesiastes 3:1, NIV tells us: *"There is a time for everything, and a season for every activity under heaven."* Some translations use the word "purpose" instead of season. They both fit with what I am saying to you at this moment. In this lifetime, you will experience many seasons, and loneliness will be one of them. However, it will be for only a season and it *will* serve a purpose.

So what purpose could your present loneliness possibly serve? It is how you *deal* with your loneliness that will serve you. The way you find solutions to your loneliness now will have a direct correlation to how you will cope with loneliness in future relationships or marriage.

If it is your aim that when you get married your new spouse will totally fill the void in your life, and you will never be lonely again, you are in for a surprise. You will find yourself putting impossible demands on that person and it will drive a wedge between the two of you. Don't get me wrong, marriage will be wonderful, but it will not be perfect. That person will not be around you all day, every day. We all have to go to jobs, out-of-state trainings, retreats, and spend time away from our spouses.

Not only that—sometimes the two of you will have disagreements in which you will feel that he or she just doesn't understand you. When that happens, you do not want to revert to old loneliness issues and fears of isolation. Improperly dealing with loneliness can lead to other emotional conditions such as control issues and neediness. These issues tend to carry a red flag everywhere they go for others to see. We all need other people, but distorted and extreme neediness tends to send people running away from us.

What are some proper ways to deal with your loneliness now, so you don't sabotage a relationship later? Here is the first step, found in Psalm 68:6, NIV: *"God sets the lonely in families ..."* Family can be anything. It could be a new job with great friends, it could be a circle of friends from your church, or it could be a group of neighbors on your block that love to get together. But you need to ask God to place you in a family. As a very wise man in my church once told me, "The Kingdom of God is built on relationships." We need people because that is how God works—through people. And a little side note here; some of the people that I wasn't exactly crazy about turned out to be the *very* people God used to bless me after I opened up and got to know them better. We cannot run from people or let past mistrust issues block us from relating to others. We need our friends and we have to be proactive about seeking them out.

I am well acquainted with the feeling of just wanting to drown your sorrows in a dark room with no one else around. I remember very well hearing my phone ring and letting the answering machine get it because I didn't want to talk to anyone. It seems that when we've been hurt, our instincts tell us to get away from everyone and withdraw. We want to play tough and say, "I don't need anyone." However, that just isolates us more and sends us deeper into loneliness.

I remember the day that I brought this issue to God. I had just started attending church again after I had stopped going for six months because of the party scene I had been involved in. (It's hard to go to church with a hangover, although, I did do it a few times). I knew I was through with that old life, but I also knew I desperately needed new, solid, fruitful friendships to keep me linked to church. My best friend attended the same church, but she was involved in ministries and couldn't hold my hand everywhere I went.

One Sunday while the preacher was preaching, I was inwardly discussing this with God. After the closing prayer, we were dismissed and I walked out of the service, alone as usual. As I walked down the hallway I clearly said to God under my breath, "God, if you want me to keep coming, I'm gonna need some friends here."

He agreed. We need other people. He said it himself in Genesis: *"It is not good that man should be alone."* He knew I was going to ask Him that and He had already prepared.

I entered the atrium area of our church. It's a large, open area with a coffee bar, bookstore, and plenty of tables and comfy chairs for fellowship. I nervously looked around, wanting to linger just a little. I knew that if I wanted new friends I was going to have to roll up my sleeves and dive in somewhere.

Then, right in front of me, I saw a woman that I had known from my college days. I recognized her immediately, but thought in my heart, "She probably wouldn't even remember me."

Usually I wouldn't be so brave as to go re-introduce myself to someone, but a voice inside me said, "Here's your first new friend." God was clearly trying to guide me. I took the challenge, walked across the room to her, and let me tell you, my stomach was in knots! She glanced in my direction and saw me approaching. Her face registered "no recollection."

"Oh great! *Awkward!*" I thought. I wanted to just pull the plug on this whole plan, but it was too late, she had seen me and I had to go through with it now. When I reached her, I told her who I was and how I had known her years ago at another church. Then a wonderful thing happened— she remembered!

We began reminiscing while asking each other things like, "Whatever happened to …" and "What are you doing now?" We quickly decided that we needed to have lunch to catch up, and bless her heart, we met that week. It turned out that *she* really needed a friend to talk to because of a hard situation that she was going through. It was something that I could give her advice on because I had experience in that area. We are friends to this day.

My circle of friends began to grow and I began to feel like I had a place in my church and it all started because I asked the Lord to supply me with friends. *He sets the lonely in families ...*

You may be saying, "That's a sweet story, but how about the Saturday nights I spend at home alone while everyone else is out on a date? Or how about the weekends I have to send my kids to the ex's and I'm left in an empty house?" Yes, I know. Been there, and been there. This is where we begin another season in our lives. Seedtime and harvest.

Remember, God said that as long as the Earth remains, there would always be seedtime and harvest. He's not just talking about crops. We sow seeds of love, hatred, friendship, prosperity, kindness, and a host of other things. Everything starts from a seed. God said in Genesis 1, everything produces after its own kind. If you want to reap a harvest of relationships, you will most definitely have to plant some seeds in that area. I didn't create the laws of the universe, I'm just reporting what they are.

So if you want to be busy on Saturday nights what should you do? Sow into someone else's Saturday nights. Offer to take a friend out to dinner. Ask someone to go to the walking trails with you Saturday evening. If you need help coping when your kids spend the weekend at your ex's, start helping someone else with the same problem. Pray for them and give them a call when it's their weekend. Whatever you wish to reap a harvest in, sow some seeds. Let God use your loneliness and availability to help other people.

Some seasons in our lives are so busy that we can close God out. For a short time during your lonely season, you just may be the only available person God can find to help someone else, and I can assure you; no one will come to you. You must go to them. You must plant your own seeds.

I love sowing seeds. I sow everywhere for all kinds of harvests. When I became a divorce recovery facilitator, I began sowing seeds into other people's healing. I was also sowing into the success of their future relationships. As a parent, I began sowing seeds into other parent's children. I directed a small children's ensemble and gave rides to church for my sons' classmates. I also took it upon myself to pray for the sons of other parents in my town. When I decided to stand by my friend who had cancer, I was sowing seeds of my own to have friends that would stand by me in hard situations. I started reaping some harvests immediately, some of them are just coming in, and some of them will come in their due season—harvest time. But, they will come in.

There is one other important area of sowing that I must cover with you. As someone who once had a "past," I spent several years anxious to have that past buried and gone forever. However, despite my good behavior, sometimes it would rear it's ugly head and surface. I soon realized why. Many times in the Bible God says, *"Love covers a multitude of sins."* I had not learned this important principle yet and sometimes found myself *exposing* other people's sins instead of covering them. Consequently, I noticed that the turn-around time for my harvest of revealing the sins of others came back to me very fast. Usually within a few days of un-covering someone's sin, something horrible from my past would haunt me. It didn't take me long at all to see the connection and rectify my folly. If I wanted my *own* sins covered, I had to learn to cover other people's sins. When I began to work this spiritual law in my life, the results were amazing!

All of this must be done in the spirit of love, not just to receive something back. As Jesus said, *"Love others as yourself."* If you love yourself enough to want to be healed of all your past relationships, then love your neighbor, too, and help them with their own journeys. The rewards will come back in a huge harvest.

If you want help from God to combat your loneliness, ask—don't complain, just ask. He said, *"You have not, because you* ask *not."* So, ask!

. . . weeping may remain for a night, but rejoicing comes in the morning. (Psalm 30:5, NIV)

CHAPTER SIXTEEN

Those Crazy Button Pushers!

Learning how to deal with button pushers is one of the greatest lessons you can learn as a single person. Why? Oh, I'm so glad you asked! I don't want to burst your fantasy love bubble, but when you get married, your other half will most likely, in some way, push some of your buttons, even if they don't mean to.

There are only two responses to having your buttons pushed:

1. You respond like a vending machine. Someone pushes the right button and you deliver the goods—words of retaliation and defense wrapped in a nice plastic smile.

2. You get rid of the buttons.

As an experienced vending machine, I can tell you many stories of having had my buttons pushed. People could easily walk up to me and push B-1, and out came my pre-programmed responses. Usually those responses were only intended to defend myself, but they usually ended up inflaming the situation. They were harsh responses full of venom, sarcasm, withdrawal, and arrogance.

Awhile back, I had the enlightening experience of being thrust into a workplace with a person that I would call a "challenging personality." My first instinct is usually to run from this kind of person and avoid them at all costs. Sometimes this isn't such a bad idea if you are trying to avoid constant confrontation. But the inability to totally avoid her made me realize that God wanted me to stop running and learn to deal with challenging people.

Day after day, this person came to my office and pushed my buttons. As a self-proclaimed, champion debater, she tried many times to ensnare me in a juicy debate of hot topics usually related to religion. I told her many times, in the most diplomatic way I could, that I could not get involved in those discussions and I had work to do. Most times, she eventually left my office, but never without a last word intended to remind me of her supremacy in the word-war arena. I was usually left in a distracted and angry state for hours. I was angered that a so-called fellow Christian would try so hard to engage me in senseless arguments.

One day as I was praying to God and whining about my "button pusher," He sweetly said to my soul, "Why is it that she can so *easily* push your buttons?" This caused some significant reflection on my part. He had a great point. We live in a world full of button pushers. Some of them are intentional and some of them are unintentional, hapless people who accidentally cross our paths on our moody days. Nevertheless, every day brings new opportunities for people to walk up to our vending machine and push a button. Typically, button pushers love bright, shiny, buttons, they are attracted to them. The only way to deal with this is to remove the buttons.

The question was left up to me. Would I be a vending machine forever? And what about my future mate? What about those days when we're all a little thin-skinned and a careless word can unwittingly provoke another, then another? How would that hurt my marriage? The Lord was right—I had to get a handle on this now.

There are two areas of our lives that we need to address in order to get rid of our vending machine buttons. The first is to pray for our button pushers. Something happens when we put down our own egos and obediently do something that does not come naturally for us. It is not natural to pray for someone that has just made you intensely angry. Trust me, it is *not* natural and it does not *feel* natural, so don't think that you have to wait to be in the mood to pray for that person because most likely, that mood will never come. You just have to do it. God knows that you don't feel like praying for that person, so you don't have to even pretend like you are really concerned about them. Just take the first step, a faith step, open your mouth, and He will do the rest.

Usually, after I have started out with my usual dry requests for God to bless that person, God starts to melt my heart slowly. Sometimes, if I will allow Him enough time, He will give me spiritual insight into that person's life and let me see his or her own insecurities and hurts. Then it all makes sense. It's not about me; it's about their need for someone to pray for them. And I'm the person He has called to do just that. I am working for the kingdom, overcoming evil with God. I'm on the right side when I pray for my enemies and they are being freed from bondages that I don't even see. Isn't this something you would want to do for your mate?

God showed me that this challenging co-worker was really trying to get my attention. She wanted to be friends with me and although her technique was a little less than charming, it was the only way she knew to engage in conversation with me in the hope that we would become friends. After God showed me that, it was easier to open up to her and allow myself some time to get to know her. This was all confirmed one day when she told me about the horrible atrocities she endured as a child. She just needed some acceptance from someone.

The second way to get rid of our buttons is to ignore the distractions in our life. Life is full of distractions, and button pushers are nothing but a distraction intended to get us off course. The Lord showed me this picture:

As Jesus was on the Cross, there were people everywhere cursing Him, challenging Him, and trying to push His buttons. His weren't the only buttons they were trying to push. Think about his mother, standing lovingly at the foot of the Cross, having to listen to insult after insult heaped on her innocent, dying Son. Do you think she might have been angry? Did any of these people push her buttons? Probably. But did she leave the foot of the Cross? No.

I am sure that she never said a word to them, but just looked intently at her Son for hours. She just wanted to be there, and not all the fury of hell would rob her of her love and devotion to stay at His side. Maybe after an hour or so, all the cruelty around her just became a low hum in her ears, just noise in the background that she hardly noticed anymore. Her eyes were on her Son and she was able to hear every soft word He spoke. She ignored the chaos around her and stayed with Jesus to the end ... to His very last breath.

If I were there, I would have been so busy running around putting everyone in his place that I would have missed the event of the ages.

We have to leave the distractions in the background, stay focused on Jesus, and the people He has given us to love and pray for. When we master this, our buttons become indistinct and button pushers lose their interest in them. No buttons—no button pushers.

As you are practicing to be a good mate, this is an area that will require a lot of dedication and commitment to change. It will also require a lot of testing before you finally begin do this with ease. However, after you pass that first test, you will feel the pleasure of finally being able to be in control of your anger and emotions and some day someone special will find that you are a keeper!

In Those Times of Doubt

When you get into a tight place and everything goes against you, until it seems as though you could not hold on a minute longer, never give up then, for that is just the time and place that the tide will turn.

– HARRIET BEECHER STOWE

CHAPTER SEVENTEEN

When God Comes on the Scene

I have loved the Bible since I was a teenager. Those Old Testament stories are like an addiction for me, but it took me years to discover one underlying theme of the Bible that helped me make sense of all the disappointments and setbacks in my life: *you can't experience a miracle until you need one!*

If life were always perfect, we would have no need for God's supernatural intervention in the situations of our lives. We would have cushioned lives with loads of money, perfect relationships, perfect jobs, and perfect kids. Of course, we would still believe in God, but would not necessarily need Him for anything except to oversee our world to make sure it was always running smoothly.

But it's not like that. Our lives are full of scares, thrills, adventures, drama, lost loves, and economic problems, bad relationships, disappointments, and life-changing events— all of which God can handle with His little finger.

As you read through the Bible, you'll notice that God's greatest and most glorious feats were performed when people were in a bind, against the wall, and in dire straits. His most famous miracle—the parting of the Red Sea—was especially exciting!

Millions of liberated Israelite slaves, who had just exited Egypt, were encamped along the Red Sea on their way to their Promised Land. When suddenly, behind them appeared the Egyptians who had decided they really did not want to lose those slaves and manual laborers so easily. It appeared that they were closing in to attack them, but God sent the Angel of the Lord to the rear of the Israelites to form a barrier to prevent the Egyptians from getting nearer. However, the Israelites still feared for their lives.

Women were alarmed, frightened children were holding onto their mothers, and the worried men were sweating, blaming, and lashing out at Moses for their predicament. But don't forget, the Angel of the Lord was between the armies of Egypt and Israel, and God was holding off the enemy. I wonder if, when the Israelites were crying out to God before the sea parted, God was softy saying, "Hold on children ... I've got you ... don't worry, you won't be hurt ... you are in store for a real treat ... you are going to see My great and mighty power make a way for you before your eyes!"

But the Israelites were still afraid. They were accusing Moses of taking them out to the desert to die. They even said they would have rather stayed in Egypt and lived out their lives as slaves than to die in the desert. Imagine that! *Wanting to go back to slavery.*

Thank God, Moses had faith in God and kept his head. He answered the people and said, "Do not be afraid. Stand firm and you will see the deliverance the Lord will bring you today. The Egyptians you see today, you will never see again. The Lord will fight for you; you need only to be still."

Then, what happened? God instructed Moses to raise his staff toward the sea and the sea parted. The Israelites crossed over safely and as the Egyptians attempted to follow suit, they all drowned as God caused the sea to close up over them. There it is, one of the greatest miracles the world has ever known, prompted by the Israelites need to be delivered.

So, why did God wait until the Israelites were cornered against the sea? Why didn't He just kill all the Egyptian soldiers back in the city? Or maybe create another plague in which all the soldiers died while the Israelites were safe in their beds? Maybe the Egyptian armies could have had an outbreak of measles or leprosy. Why get the Israelites into a position in which it appeared they were about to lose their freedom and possibly their lives?

Why? So that God could work a miracle and be unmistakably glorified here on the Earth. It simply means that He, in His innate glory and goodness, desires to bring His light and self-revelation to mankind. And mankind desperately needs to see God!

A miracle is a moment in time when God gets to show the world His heart and love for His people through a significant, supernatural event. God thrusts His head through the curtain of the heavenly realm and enters the physical world, so that we can see Him and gain understanding of who He is. He does something that no earthly person could possibly accomplish so there is no misunderstanding about His power or His authority. His children can witness the fact that they really can trust Him and that He always prevails.

His desire to reveal himself to His children is incredibly strong. He will work in your situation to show you, and those around you, that He is the one and only, true, undisputable, undeniable God, and you are safe in His hands!

There are several things we can draw out of this story that will help us keep our heads together until God delivers us from our trouble.

1) Don't even *think* of going back to Egypt. Egypt represents everything that you were enslaved to before— alcohol, drugs, sex, bad relationships, habits, etc.... If you get tempted to want to go back to any of those things, just remember the costs; Egypt always demands more than you can give, costs more than you have, and takes you further than you want to go. Do not go there.

2) Stand firm. Have an expectant hope that God is on His way to deliver you, because He is. Don't just rely on what you can see with your eyes. God is always working behind the scenes to bring your deliverance at just the right time.

3) Be confident that you are not trapped. God can open a path right through your sea of problems and see you safely to the other side. The same sea that seemed like a barrier to the Israelites actually became the instrument that freed them and killed the Egyptians. Your liability can become your opportunity when you give it to God. Amazing, isn't it?

4) Know that God can supernaturally hold off your enemies until you are fully delivered. He still erects

boundaries today and those boundaries are as powerful as a wall of fire.

5) Although this was a frightening scene for the Israelites, it needed to happen in order to rid them of the Egyptians forever. Had the Israelites escaped another way, without going through the sea, they would have forever been looking over their shoulders for those dreaded Egyptians. Trust God's wisdom, He knows how to deal with your enemies so that they can never threaten you again.

6) The fact that you need a miracle puts you in the position to receive one. So get excited, you are about to see something you have never seen before!

During my years as a single person, I have derived much help and wisdom from this story. When my finances were in shambles and I thought the creditors were about to take my house and car, God assured me that He could, and would, hold off my creditors until I could get back on my feet and work things out with them. I never lost anything. When my safety felt threatened as a single woman, I remembered that He puts a hedge between me and those that threaten me.

Whenever I was tempted to go back to my old ways—Egypt—God gave me the strength to not look back, and the hope to look forward to my Promised Land. If I was tempted to fear in a situation, I realized God knew exactly where I was and He would not allow me to be hurt. When I wondered, "What is this all for?" He reminded me that He would be glorified through the events in my life and I would be a hope and example for others. Most importantly, when I found myself in a difficult situation that no earthly person could help me with, I got excited and thought to myself, "This is a perfect setup for God to work a miracle. Wonder what He's going to do?"

I began to look at the desperate situations in my life in a new light, seeing them as a real chance to watch God do something crazy, exciting, and creative. He has definitely come through and shown me some great and supernatural answers to my prayers.

Do not let any situation convince you that your back is against a wall, because I assure you, God can make that wall come tumbling down. Believe Him, trust Him, and look for everything to be possible in your life. Everything!

CHAPTER EIGHTEEN

How Will I Ever Meet Someone?

When I was in college, I had a job as a sales consultant for a well-known chain of diamond jewelry stores and stayed in that profession for eight years. Although I didn't particularly love the pressure of meeting sales quotas, I did come to truly love meeting people. When you are selling diamonds to people, especially their engagement rings and anniversary bands, it's wonderful to find out about them as couples and their relationships. I loved hearing their stories and I was never shy about asking, "How did you meet?"

I asked almost everyone, from the young couples just engaged, to older married couples who were celebrating years of wedded bliss. I loved how their stories were always unique, never the same. Some began with love at first sight, while others started out as friends. Some knew instantly that the other person was "the one," while others needed more time to cultivate a friendship and finally a romance.

There were a few parallels, though. They usually met through friends, work, hobbies, school, church, or other similar interests. Interestingly enough, a huge percentage of them weren't consciously looking for a mate when "theirs truly" showed up. I don't recall anyone saying, "Oh, everywhere I went I was looking for a mate. I looked at the grocery store, at the movie theatre, up and down the rows at church, at the gas station, at the bars ... my eyes were always peeled looking for the one." Although, it may be true that some of them did do those things, they eventually met someone through a repeated activity or a relationship with others.

I say this, so that you can relax a little if you are one of the ones looking everywhere you go. You probably won't run into a convenience store to pay for your gas and come out with a new, potential mate. Okay, maybe there are a *few* of those "grocery store" stories, but *very* few of them. And to be honest, I've been a little creeped out a few times when a perfect stranger approached me with a cheesy pick-up line in the produce section.

I find all my answers in the Bible, so I must find the answer to this perplexing question there too. How will I meet someone? Two of my favorite *single-woman-meets-her-husband* stories were those of Ruth and Rebekah.

In the Book of Ruth, we find that Ruth was a loyal and faithful friend to Naomi, her mother-in-law, even after both of them had lost their husbands. Although she could have abandoned her widowed mother-in-law to search for another husband for herself, she chose to stay with Naomi and care for her as she would her own mother. Because Ruth showed such loyalty to Naomi, word got around of what a faithful and good person she was.

To provide food for both of them, Ruth went to the wheat fields every day hoping to glean a small portion of the grain left behind by the harvesters. When Boaz, the owner of the field, noticed her hard work and asked about her, the townspeople had plenty of good things to say about her. He was impressed. All of this was going on while she was minding her own business working in the fields, oblivious that anyone had even noticed her.

Let's just stop right here for a moment. Someone could be noticing you right now and you aren't even aware of it. They could be gaining more interest in you as they begin to ask around to hear what kind of person you are. What are they hearing about you? Are they hearing that you are loyal, faithful, and a good worker? Can they observe you loving and serving people? Or do they see you being short with checkers in checkout lines, snapping at people, and treating your own family badly? It's a good question for all of us to ask ourselves.

Getting back to the story, I'll give you the short version. Boaz showed great kindness to Ruth and favored her. When Naomi got wind of it, she was ecstatic. She wanted the best for this daughter-in-law of hers and Boaz was a well-known, respected man of the community. Moreover, he was a kinsman redeemer—a close relative that could take responsibility for Naomi's late husband's estate. Naomi knew that Boaz was a great man of character and would redeem her estate. He did; he took responsibility for Naomi, *and* he married Ruth. He was extremely pleased to be able to marry Ruth. Together they had a child that became the grandfather to the great King David, and all because Ruth was loyal to her mother-in-law.

The story of Rebekah and Isaac, in the Book of Genesis, shows us that God times the events in our lives for many reasons. In this case, Isaac's mother, Sarah, had just died and the whole family was in mourning. Isaac was single and had been the light of his mother's life. Since we know that she didn't have him until she was ninety years old, I'm sure that their relationship was quite special as this aging woman, no doubt, wanted to make the most of every day with her son.

After she died, Abraham, Isaac's father, decided it was time for Isaac to get married and sent a servant to go fetch a wife for him. He did not want his son to marry a pagan or someone that did not have the same beliefs, so he instructed the servant to go back to Abraham's own homeland and people.

It is the same with your heavenly Father. He doesn't want you to be linked with someone that is entirely different spiritually or morally. He wants to you have the best and He knows just what town he or she lives in. (He knows *your* address too, by the way.)

So the servant saddled up and went to find a wife for Isaac. That's a lot of pressure—finding a wife for your master—and the servant was obviously *feeling* the pressure, too. He prayed fervently that God would give him success and lead him to the right woman for Isaac.

As he approached the designated town where he was to find a wife, he specifically prayed that as he stopped at a well to drink, God would show him the chosen woman by her willingness to give him a drink, and also offering to water his camels. He hadn't even finished praying when pretty little Rebekah came on the scene with her jar to fetch some water.

He asked her if she would draw some water for him and she answered, "Of course, and I'll draw water for your camels too." As she ran back and forth fetching water for his camels until they were satisfied, the servant must have been astonished. The first girl he talked to. This was easy! When she told him that she belonged to the family of his master Abraham, he bowed down and worshipped the Lord right then and there.

Let's take a moment to examine this. I see a pattern here. Rebekah seems to be another young girl who is not only a good worker, but goes beyond the call of duty to help someone. Watering a group of camels is no easy task— they can drink forever. But Rebekah was generous in spirit and offered her help without reservation. The man she was helping was not a rich young ruler; he was just a servant. However, you just never know what kind of connections the people you speak to have. As she's working her sweet little legs off for this man, she has no idea that he's thinking, "She might be the one!" The Bible says that without saying a word, he watched her closely the whole time to learn if the Lord had made his journey successful.

Sisters, I think I can safely say that most men notice you long before you notice them. They notice. And brothers, I think I can safely say to you that if you ask the Lord to bring a likely candidate to your attention, He will do it. I would even go so far as to say that you could ask for a particular quality to stand out to you. It happened in the Bible and God has not changed in the last few thousand years. The important thing is that both parties were busy. Rebekah was drawing water for her family and the servant was busy about his master's business. These people weren't holed up in their houses perusing the Internet looking for chat rooms for singles. They were out in the world helping people, serving their families, and making a difference.

Back to the story. Again, to make a long story short, Rebekah agreed to go back with the servant to marry Isaac. I love this next part—it's like a scene from a movie. I can't tell it as well as God does, so here is the passage from Genesis 24:61-67, NIV:

> Then Rebekah and her maids got ready and mounted their camels and went back with the man. So the servant took Rebekah and left.
>
> Now Isaac had come from Beer Lahai Roi, for he was living in the Negev. He went out to the field one evening to meditate, and as he looked up, he saw camels approaching. Rebekah also looked up and saw Isaac. She got down from her camel and asked the servant, "Who is that man in the field coming to meet us?"
>
> "He is my master," the servant answered. So she took her veil and covered herself. Then the servant told Isaac all he had done. Isaac brought her into the tent of his mother Sarah, and he married Rebekah. So she became his wife and he loved her; and Isaac was comforted after his mother's death.

God's timing is perfect! Rebekah came along at just the right time. Isaac had a hole in his heart from the passing of his mother and Rebekah was a gift from God that healed his broken heart. His love and appreciation for her must have been pure bliss.

I personally love this story because the first time Rebekah laid eyes on Isaac, he was out in the field meditating, seeking God. Nothing is as attractive as a man who spends time seeking God for guidance in his life. It's exactly the kind of man I want to meet.

Let's recap some of the things we have learned from these two stories:

- It is important for us singles to be people of character and integrity. People notice, word gets around, and someone could be watching you right now.

- Treat your family with loyalty and honor. God doesn't want to send you a mate whom you will treat badly. Your new mate will become family.

- Get out of seclusion and start helping people. Get active in church, charities, and good causes. Look after others and God will look after you.

- Treat everyone the same regardless of their status. The lowly servant that you are kind to might want to introduce you to his boss!

- Don't be afraid to get specific about the kind of person you want to meet. In that way, you are giving God something to work with.

- God is timing your meeting so that the circumstances are just right for both of you. You will both be a huge blessing to each other when it happens.

- Until that person comes along, spend time with God, seeking Him, and meditating on Him. Your new mate will love being the answer to your prayers.

As we have seen in both stories, sometimes the ball starts rolling long before we are aware of it. The idea is that it is more important to *be* the right person than it is to *find* the right person. Position yourself so that you will be a blessing to the one you meet, and most of all trust God. He can make it all happen.

CHAPTER NINETEEN

You Can, You Must, and You Will!

I had a dream about you one night. I dreamed you were standing in a field and there were hundreds of little snakes all around you. They were small, but very annoying. A snake would jump on you, and you would shake it off. Then another would wrap around your leg and you would kick it off. Then another would land on your shoulders and you flipped it off with your hand. A few seconds would pass and you thought they were finally going to leave you alone, but then another clamped down on your hand and you violently flung it away. The more the snakes came at you, the harder you fought and the more determined you became to conquer them. As hard as they tried, they could not stay on you without your fighting them off. As soon as one latched on, you powerfully threw it off. You never gave up and they never conquered you. You kept fighting. Then I woke up.

The next night I dreamed about you again. You were on the front porch of a house facing a yard with a white picket fence around it and the yard was full of scorpions. You were locked out of the house and needed to get out of the yard to the safety of the street. You carefully began to maneuver through the yard. You thoughtfully chose each step, careful not to stir up any of the scorpions. You would see a patch of grass with no scorpions and take a step. Then you would look for another clear spot and take another step. The scorpions just roamed along the ground ignoring you. As you took each step, you neared the safety of the street. Finally, you took your final step, exited to the street, and slammed the gate shut behind you with a sigh of relief and a sense of amazement.

A few nights later, I dreamed about you again. You and several other people were caught in a flooded river and were being swept along by the powerful current. Your head easily remained above water as the current pushed you further down the river. The other people in the river were floating along beside you. As the current began to slow, you could see that there was a huge rock in front of you. You knew that if you could reach the rock you would avoid being swept all the way downstream with the others. As you approached the rock, you put your hands out and clung to it. The current was gentler at this point and didn't pull you away from the rock. You then began to feel around the bottom of the riverbed with your feet to see how deep the water was. To your surprise, you were over a shallow sand bar and could stand up in the river. Other people slowly passed you, as they remained content to float with current of the river. You slowly began to make your way to the bank.

I read a story that reminded me of you. A woman and her son were walking through a desert. They had been cast out of their family and sent to the desert with only what they could carry. As the days passed, they ran out of water. As the woman looked to the horizon she could see no end, no relief, just endless desert. The woman could feel her will to live slowly draining. Finally, she could go no further. It was time to give up. She couldn't bear the thought of seeing her son die before her eyes, so she placed him under a bush and then found a spot several yards away so that she could close her eyes and die too. She began to sob as she heard the soft cries of her child. Then she heard a voice that said to her, "Do not be afraid, God has heard the boy crying as he lies there. Lift the boy up and take him by the hand, for I will make him into a great nation." Then she opened her eyes and saw a well of water.

I had one final dream about you. You and your family were in your house when suddenly, you heard tornado warning sirens in the distance. As you ran to your window to see what was going on, you could see the winds around your house were becoming violent, trees were bending wildly, and the sky was getting dark. You sent your family to a safe place in your home, but you yourself remained in front of the window. From deep inside yourself, you began to cry to God for help. As you kept crying and praying, you could see the home next to you begin to tear apart. Bricks were ripping from the house and swirling in the air. Just then, your attention was drawn to something beautiful. A large, stunning, brightly colored bird flew to your window. The bird looked straight at you and peace was in its eyes. Somehow, you knew that the bird was a messenger from God and your house would not be harmed. The bird flew away, the wind died down, and your family was safe.

Perseverance: To persist in anything undertaken; maintain a purpose in spite of difficulty, obstacles, or discouragement; continue steadfastly.

Perseverance seems to be a forgotten character trait among people today, but it is something that you can develop with a new attitude and some resolve. Whether you are feeling so lonely you want to die, or whether it just seems like everything in your life is going wrong, you must decide that you will persevere. When you feel waves of depression sweeping over you, you must keep fighting, and reach out to the rock. You must resist the desire to just be swept along against your will. You must keep fighting off those snakes and you must be brave enough to walk through a yard of scorpions to reach your destination.

I know it's hard. I know there are days you just want to stay in bed and hide from the world. I've been there. Whenever I faced hard times in the past, I used to wish I could be like a bear and hibernate until spring came around and hope was in the air again. I think that mentally, I *did* hibernate sometimes. I didn't even have a lick of perseverance in me. When things got tough, I ran away from friends, jobs, relationships, financial crises, and anything else that reared its ugly head. Once things got uncomfortable, I was outta there.

But the truth is, that is just not God's way. God doesn't always remove us from our troubles. Sometimes He takes us *through* them, and for good reason, I might add. Our ability to persevere is incredibly important to God. He made that clear in the James 1:2-4, NIV:

Consider it pure joy, my brothers, whenever you face trials of many kinds, because you know that the testing of your faith develops perseverance. Perseverance must finish its work so that you may be mature and complete, not lacking anything.

In other words, if we haven't developed perseverance, God considers us incomplete and immature in our faith. God loves us too much to leave us that way. Therefore, like a mother bird, He moves us to the edge of the nest and with a gentle push, He forces us to fly and grow up. A test or trial comes along and He allows us to face it. No more hiding, no more procrastinating, no more running away. It is time to face the winds of life and realize that they are actually the very things that will strengthen us. This time you have to go through the trial and keep going until you reach the end.

Three years ago, I was in a terrible car accident and broke several bones in my face. At the scene of the accident, panic was in the air, and I saw my son crying as he looked at me. I began to wonder what had happened to my face. Within seconds, a woman appeared at my side. She was a nurse who had happened upon the wreck. She saw my fear and gently pulled my head to face her as she sternly said to me, "Look at me. You are going to get through this and you will be fine."

That is what I'm saying to you right now. Whatever your situation, you are going to get through it, and you will be fine. You will not die, you will get stronger. If you feel that you are in a financial desert and there is no way out, you must trust that God will supply your needs and can still make you into something great. If you are feeling rejected by friends, family, or a past lover, you must stay strong and persevere. You can, you must, and you will persevere.

Your ability to persevere through the hard times will be the glue that keeps you and your future mate together so you won't become a statistic. Your attitude of perseverance will give your mate confidence and a sense of safety in your relationship. Your commitment to never give up will be the inspiration your children will need to pursue their own goals and relationships. You will be unique, priceless, courageous, and Christ-like because you can persevere to the very end.

God has already decided the number of days you will live on this Earth and He has already provided everything you will need to fulfill each of those days. His mercy is new every morning and He longs to show you compassion. Every day you will be provided with enough grace to get you through, enough grace for the whole day, every day.

When you feel that you are in a desert and there is no hope, He will come to you, strengthen you, and He will be a well of water to you. When you feel that something is trying to sweep you away like a tornado, call out to God, He will help you. Just decide now that you are going to be a person who perseveres.

Fear not, for I have redeemed you; I have summoned you by name; you are mine. When you pass through the waters, I will be with you; and when you pass through the rivers, they will not sweep over you. When you walk through the fire, you will not be burned; the flames will not set you ablaze. For I am the LORD, your God, the Holy One of Israel, your Savior. (Isaiah 43:1-3, NIV)

CHAPTER TWENTY

Why Am I Waiting on God Anyway?

Just to let you know that the single life is always a work in progress, let me share something that happened to me one weekend several months ago.

I, Stacy, the one who has it all together (right!), had one of those "moments." I was feeling lonely one evening and I felt tears come to my eyes. I'm just like anyone else who feels the pain of loneliness. I have wonderful sons who are a joy to live with, but they are getting older now and are usually off to the bowling alley or a movie with a carload of friends, leaving me alone to fend for myself for the evening.

Although I usually have plenty of activities and friends to pal around with on the weekends, this particular weekend I had been mostly alone. I had gone to a Friday night church service and ended up sitting by myself. The next day I watched my son play baseball and sat alone in the stands. That night I had been invited to a surprise birthday party and had a nice time, but left by myself and drove home alone. My "moment" hit on the car ride home.

I began asking out loud, "What am I doing all this for? I could be dating up a storm right now! I could go to nice restaurants and have wonderful dates with some guy—any guy. I could have someone calling me to ask me how my day had gone. I could have someone to sit by me at my son's basketball games while my ex-husband sits with his new girlfriend in the stands in front of me. Other people are dating. Why am I not dating? Where's *my* man?" My faith was being tested and I knew that I could not let my mind roam. I had to go to my Bible.

I began reading in 2 Chronicles, one of my favorite books of the Bible. I was inspired, but I still felt numb and I did not have an answer yet. The Holy Spirit moved me to go to the Song of Solomon.

"Why in the world do I want to read the *love* book right now?" I asked out loud. "As if I'm not lonely enough! Like I really need to read about Solomon and the Shulammite woman longing for each other with unquenchable desire." Yet, I felt that I should obey, so I began reading.

The Song of Solomon is actually a love story about Jesus and His adoration for us, the bride of Christ. It's hard not to fall in love with Jesus when reading this. He wants to have such an intimate relationship with us. *"My beloved is mine, and I am his."* He is so beautiful. I could feel my heart finding peace and love because of the words I was reading. I was reading of Jesus' love for me straight from His heart as He said, *"You have captivated my heart, my sister, my bride."*

As I was finishing the book, I paused on the verse in which we find the bride saying, *"I adjure you, oh daughters of Jerusalem, that you not stir up or awaken love until it pleases"* (Song of Solomon 8:4, ESV). It's a verse I have read many times, and have heard speakers give explanations of what the bride meant by that verse. The most popular view is that she is saying, "Don't play with fire until you've got your own fireplace at home"... or something similar to that. I closed my Bible thinking about how I would love to meet someone with the wisdom of Solomon. I didn't quite have the answer to why I hadn't met my man yet, but I felt better and I felt my love for Jesus renewed and even intensified.

The next day I attended the Sunday evening service at my church. After the services were over, I slowly exited my row of seats. I was still a little quiet; still pondering the question I had been asking the night before. One of my friends called out to me and wanted to walk out with me. As we greeted each other, I asked her how she was doing. She was obviously a little sad and replied, "I'm okay, but I've had a very hard week." Tears were forming in her eyes.

"What's going on?" I asked.

She began. "Well, I've been corresponding with this awesome guy in another state for several months. We have mutual friends that introduced us and we've been corresponding a lot over the Internet and talking a lot over the phone and decided to meet. He's just the best guy I've ever met. He's a great Christian, successful, and perfect in every way. He arranged to fly me out to where he lives and I went last weekend."

"And?" I probed.

"And, when I met him in person, I was disappointed. He wasn't quite what I had in mind. His demeanor was very different in person from what I had experienced by talking to him on the phone and I actually found him difficult to be around. My heart was broken. I had spent months getting to know him through emails and phone calls, building him up in my mind as *the one*, and it turned out he wasn't right for me at all." The tears began to flow down her cheeks as she continued.

"I wish I hadn't even met him, I'm so hurt, and I feel this great loss. Now I want to find someone more than ever. It's like this desire was aroused in me to have someone in my life and when it didn't work out, the desire didn't go away. I feel lonelier now than ever."

With impeccable timing, the Holy Spirit spoke softly in my heart, "Don't stir up or awaken love until it pleases."

A light bulb lit up above my head as I got a revelation of what the Lord had been trying to tell me. "Ohhh, I get it now," I said inwardly. And it made perfect sense.

Now I remember why I'm waiting to date. God has my life timed to the second and He's way too intelligent to waste even a moment of my life. At the right time, in the right season, when it's right for all concerned, God will bring me and my *intended* together. If I try to force something to happen before the appointed time, the end result will be worse than if I had just waited. My heart will be broken, and I will suffer great disappointment. My desires will be stirred even more to keep searching and I will find myself in a state of confusion and wondering. I don't know about you, but I don't want that.

We have a saying in Divorce Recovery: *it's better to go your whole life wanting something you don't have, than to go your whole life having something you don't want.* Boy is that ever true! There is nothing more discouraging, crushing, and disheartening than two people who are locked in an unhappy marriage, just living day in and day out, with no joy or hope for change. I am sure you have known a few of those unhappy couples. We call them married singles; two people who are married to each other but living individual lives under the same roof, unable or unwilling to work on the marriage. Those are some of the most miserable people on Earth.

Believe it or not, single sister or brother, if you feel that you are so unhappy because there is no one in your life, you are still in a far better place than those who are struggling with an unhappy marriage. It breaks God's tender, compassionate, heart to see people merely existing from day to day in unhappy circumstances. It is definitely not the *abundant* life He had in mind when He sent His Son to redeem us from the curse of the Law. In addition, it sure does not fit His definition of the blessed life. He *does* care about whom, how, and when you marry. He cares and He wants to be involved. Very involved.

Do not stir up or awaken love until it pleases. When it's right, it will definitely please. God knows us so well. He knows things about me that I don't even know about myself. He knows all the quirks and bad habits that we have. He also knows all the talents and gifts we have that can benefit someone else. He knows the right combinations of personality types that can co-exist peacefully and He knows the kind of people that will inspire us and the kind of people that will drag us down. He knows the relationships that will end up with disappointment and the ones that will grow stronger. He knows what makes us laugh and what depresses us. He wants your marriage to be successful, joyful, satisfying, and prosperous.

Some people say that they are stepping out in faith by pursuing a relationship that might be right for them. I say I am stepping out in faith by *not* pursuing anything that I am not absolutely sure is from God. It takes a lot of faith to wait. It takes a lot of faith to believe in a God that you cannot see with human eyes. It takes a lot of faith to be led by the Holy Spirit, instead of being led by our crazy emotions, but read Hebrews 11. Faith pays off, and faith turns us into better, stronger people.

I can do this! I can do this through Christ who strengthens me ... and so can you.

CHAPTER TWENTY-ONE

Our Precious Desert Experience

You are probably not going to understand what I'm about to say, but here goes: if you haven't had a desert experience yet, you do not know what you're missing. Is it the most enjoyable experience of your life? No. So why in the world would I recommend it to you? Because it is the deepest and richest growth period in your life. Your desert experience is a God-ordained season of life in which God speaks to you alone and your stake in the Christian life is either cemented or weakened. It shapes who you are and it reveals who you are. It asks, "Are you really in this for keeps, or are you just playing around?"

You cannot decide on your own that you are headed to the desert. You have to be led, just as Jesus was led to the desert right after He had been baptized in the Jordan. He didn't even get to have a baptismal, congratulatory, potluck dinner with His friends after He left the river. The Bible says He was led by the Holy Spirit straight to the desert to be tempted by the devil.

For forty days, Jesus fasted while Satan threw temptation after temptation at Him and the Bible says He was tempted in *every* way. I can only imagine the many things that the devil tried to bombard our Savior with. We know that He was tempted with things that are common to all men. Maybe the devil threw images of beautiful women in front of Jesus. Maybe he tried to suggest thoughts to Him like, "No one wants you! Here you are thirty years old and still single. All your friends have children and families now. You're a loser and your family thinks you're crazy. Maybe you're schizophrenic. What if you're sick? What if you have cancer? Haven't you noticed how tired you are lately? Have you seen how everyone looks at you? They talk about you behind your back. Why do you waste time going to temple? Those stories from the Torah aren't really true. Why does God let good people die? Don't you think if He really cared for you, your life would be perfect? "

On and on for forty days, Jesus was tempted by the Father of Lies. We know specifically that His identity as the beloved Son of God was challenged, His devotion to God and His destiny to be Savior of the world was challenged, and His ability to trust God for the safety of His life was challenged. Each time, Jesus answered with the Word. He wasn't defending Himself, His dignity, or His rights, He was defending the Word. He lived by the Word and He knew that the Word gives us life and sustains us because He *is* the *Word*.

There are many times the Bible tells us that God allowed people to be tested to see what was in their hearts. It is not only for God to see what is in your heart, but also for *you* to see what is in your heart. Why is that so important as a single person? Because the things that are in your heart now will also be in your heart when you get married, unless some changes are made. If doubt and confusion about God's

Word are in your heart now, they won't magically change when you get married. If you tend to get depressed when hard times hit, it won't be any different when you have a spouse. These things need to be discerned and dealt with now, before you are joined with another life.

So, exactly what is a desert experience and how do you know when you're having one? Here are a few indicators:

- You feel more alone, even in the presence of friends.
- Your faith is being seriously tested.
- Life is throwing some real curve balls at you.
- You seem stuck, as if life isn't moving forward, but just standing still.
- You are questioning where God is.
- It's hard to see your future right now.

If you are experiencing any of these situations in your life right now, congratulations! You are right where God wants you. Don't worry; it won't last forever, it's just for a season. However, what happens right now will determine a lot of things about your future as a single person, and possibly as a married person.

The desert is a place where we learn to truly trust in God. When the Israelites left Egypt, they were on their way to the great Promised Land but one small hindrance surfaced: they did not have any faith. They had sent twelve spies into the Promised Land but those spies came back with a bad report. They were fearful because there were giants in the land, and their lack of faith was revealed as they compared themselves to small grasshoppers in relation to those giants.

They were still acting like slaves. God had taken them out of Egypt but now He had to take the Egypt out of them. Without faith, they wouldn't be able to win any battles and they would be like sitting ducks. God could not send them anywhere until they had some faith.

They remained in the desert and faith training began immediately. They had to depend on Him for their food, provisions, health, and leadership. God provided manna for them and each day they received only enough manna for that day and no more. There was no savings account, no surplus, and no wealthy relatives in the next state, only God. Slowly, they learned to trust that God would provide for them daily and as those that had no faith died off, a new generation of Israelites grew and thrived under the supernatural hand of God's provision. After forty years, they were stronger and had been transformed into a people full of faith and trust in God. They march into their Promised Land, conquered the inhabitants, and became a great nation.

The righteous shall live by faith. This is God's design for those that follow Christ—to live by faith and *only* by faith. The righteous do not live by any other means but God alone. Sometimes it's a strange and unpredictable life but it's also exciting and rewarding. The only way to learn how to live by faith is to spend some time in the desert doing it. In time, your trust in God will multiply and you will be spiritually mature enough to progress into the next season of your life, which will probably require you to win some battles when you get there.

For right now, while you're in the desert, relax a little—your needs will be met. God will provide your manna every day. Most of that manna will be found in reading the Word of God and just as Jesus defeated the devil with the Word, so must you. Spend your days in the desert growing and stretching as you seek God's wisdom and presence. Read a chapter in the Book of Proverbs each day and grow, grow, grow. In time, you will see your lack of faith dying off as a new you emerges stronger and better. Just make sure you come out of the desert the same way that Jesus did—victorious.

When Jesus entered His desert experience, He was full of the Spirit. Luke 14 tells us that when Jesus came out of the desert, He came out in the *power* of the Spirit. He then went to the villages in this power and performed many astonishing miracles. Your desert experience serves a great purpose: to empower you, train you and inevitably bless many people around you. When you come out of your desert experience victoriously, get ready for some great rewards, not only in your life, but in the lives of those whom you touch.

What's Ahead for You?

I can tell you how to get what you want;
you've just got to keep the thing in view and go for it,
and never let your eyes wander to the right or left
or up or down. And looking back is fatal.

— WILLIAM LOCKE

CHAPTER TWENTY-TWO

Restoration Is for You!

In the Introduction of this book, I shared the verse God gave me that has been the theme song for my single life. Zechariah 9:12, GNT: "*Return, you exiles who now have hope; return to your place of safety. Now I tell you that I will repay you twice over with blessing for all you have suffered.*" This verse rang in my heart for months.

God will restore *twice* as much? *More* than I had before? I knew God was generous and that He always used words like abundance, running over, exceedingly, multiply, fruitful, and plenteous, just to name a few, but I had never applied it to my own wrecked life. I had always considered myself just to be lucky that He was nice to me and didn't hold a grudge. I didn't want to ask or expect any more than that. You know, "Beggars can't be choosers," "Be happy with what you've got," etc.

I began to study God's restoration and realized that the principle of restoration was not just a nice perk for being one of God's children; it was God's law. In the Old Testament, when someone took or destroyed something that belonged to another, God demanded that they restore

153

double, fivefold, and even sevenfold. Knowing the character of God, this was not a demand He just pulled out of the air, it is a principle He uses himself. God practices what He preaches.

As I studied the Bible, I found some great examples of God's restoration. We all know the story of Job and how he lost everything, but do you remember how he made out in the end?

> *After Job had prayed for his friends, the LORD made him prosperous again and gave him twice as much as he had before ... the LORD blessed the latter part of Job's life more than the first.* (Job 42:10-12, NIV)

Another great example of God's restoration happened in the book of Daniel. King Nebuchadnezzar was the king during the time of Daniel, one of God's servants. One day as the king was walking on the roof of the royal palace admiring the kingdom, he got a little too prideful in his heart and God needed to show him "the light." He was soon humbled and driven from his kingdom with a good dose of insanity to boot. He lived like a wild animal and ate grass like a cow for seven years. However, at the end of seven years, he looked up to Heaven, acknowledged God as the Most High and his sanity was restored. However, that was not all the restoration he received, in the following verse, we see how God worked restoration in his life.

> *At the same time that my sanity was restored, my honor and splendor were returned to me for the glory of my kingdom. My advisors and nobles sought me out, and I was restored to my throne and became even greater than before.* (Daniel 4:36, NIV)

King Nebuchadnezzar's receivevd back his kingdom, he regained his sanity, and he was restored in the eyes of the people around him. He became greater than he was before.

God spoke to me one day as I drove my regular route to work. He wanted to show me what His restoration looks like. I had always passed by a familiar house in an upscale suburban community. This house had burned down to the ground several years earlier. It was quite the news for our community, given the size and elegance of the house. As a fire engulfed the home, the family had escaped to safety, but the house was left in ashes. Only a few walls were left standing and the interior was completely gutted. What was once a beautiful home that passersby envied had been reduced to a black, useless heap of ashes.

A few months after the fire, it was time to rebuild. Everything was cleared down to the foundation and corrections were made to ensure a stable, erect home. As time passed, you could see contractors and workers on the site analyzing, reframing, and rebuilding. The new structure resembled the old home, but huge improvements were made this time.

The owners were able to add extras that could make their new home more enjoyable and functional than the first. Electrical outlets were placed in more inconspicuous places and taller ceilings added an air of grandeur to the home. The kitchen was greatly improved by adding more storage space and the family had fun selecting higher-end appliances for practical purposes. On the outside, newer brick and stone were used to enhance the beauty and give added value.

After months of intense labor, the finished product was a sight to behold. It was the same house, but it wasn't the same house; it was better than before. I can just imagine the first night the owners spent in their new home, how clean everything felt, and how wonderful it was to be among their neighbors again.

This is how God plans to restore your life and mine. He first clears out all the old debris and sometimes this is a long task as He eliminates old thought patterns, toxic friendships, spending habits, vices, and guilt from past mistakes. He has to get down to a clean foundation so that He can start all over. Without clearing the old foundation first, it would be like putting new carpet down on the old charred carpet of the house.

Then He starts to rebuild and a new frame begins to take shape. Faith is stronger, new relationships are blooming, and healthier habits are forming. People start taking notice that you seem different. They even make statements like, "I can see you growing through this," or "You seem calmer lately."

Truthfully, it takes a while to rebuild and can be painfully slow. Rome wasn't built in a day, that's for sure. God takes a lot of time to make sure everything is just right and nothing is left that can lead to weak spots later. He is perfecting that which concerns you.

Most people do not want to wait for God to finish rebuilding, or to build at all. They want to go ahead and move into the charred remains of their former house. Starting a relationship when you have just ended one would be like this family moving into their house while it was still just a frame with no roof or drywall. Some people are just in too much of a rush to take the time to envision all the delights and improvements that they could enjoy with a complete restoration. They want a new life *now* and that is all they can think about.

If you have just suffered a divorce, separation, or ended a long relationship, it will take some time to rebuild. Old residue will need to be cleared away and you will need to start a new foundation. I have been told that when contractors are laying the foundation for large skyscrapers, they first have to dig down several hundred feet into the earth to anchor the foundation deeply enough so that the whole building is supported against strong winds and other forces. It is absolutely essential to insure the strength and safety of a building that towers many stories above the ground. This is what God longs to do in your life. He wants to go deep and create an anchor and foundation in your life that will withstand the fiercest winds and storms. Then He wants to build your life high with many blessings. He wants to take you higher and higher. He will take you as high as you will let Him.

Give Him this. Let Him have His way. Allow Him to reconstruct your life with the new, the unfamiliar, and the better. Let Him take you out of your comfort zone and pull you into new areas of thought, belief, and friendship. When you feel that change is coming your way, embrace it and go with it. Allow Him to put you in new places in which you feel nervous, shy, and stretched. Accept invitations to fellowship with new groups of people. Let God show you a new career. Open yourself up to the Bible like a child reading it for the first time. It is all part of His wonderful plan to make you stronger, better, and more blessed than you have ever been before.

The wise man built his house upon a rock,
and the rains came tumbling down.
The rains came down as the floods came up
and the house on the rock stood firm.
The foolish man built his house upon the sand,
and the rains came tumbling down.
The rains came down as the floods came up
and the house on the sand went splat!

CHAPTER TWENTY-THREE

The Mercy of God

"This is stupid and I can't wait to move out when I'm eighteen!"

My son shouted these words at me just a couple of hours ago after a disagreement over his punishment of being grounded for the weekend. My sweet, teenaged, middle child was disrespectful to me yesterday, so I grounded him for the weekend. It's Friday afternoon and he's feeling the pains of not being able to be with his friends tonight. I'm feeling the pain with him. I really hate punishing my children.

After the discussion between my son and me calmed down somewhat, I went to my bedroom and called my best friend Kim. Best friends are great for these kinds of things, especially when those friends are full of godly wisdom. It just so happens, that she is going through the very same thing with her teenage daughter. We shared our concerns for our kids and mostly, our desire to parent our kids the way God parents us.

I want so strongly for my children to understand the ways of God through my parenting. I want to be Christ to them in my home and it is my hope that when they are adults they will want to run to their heavenly Father in all the situations of their lives and know Him as I know Him; as an amazing, merciful Father.

Kim has been reading a wonderful book about parenting and she gave me some sound wisdom.

She said, "You know, God doesn't treat us as our sins deserve and He is always full of grace and mercy."

I agreed, "Oh, you're so right! Although I've done some terrible things, when I repented and showed a broken and contrite heart to God, He showed me mercy."

"God's mercies are new each morning. Maybe our mercy should be new each morning too," she added.

"This is true," I responded. "While we've been talking I've been thinking about giving my son a chance to repent and to receive mercy. He still needs to see the grounding through today, but if he shows a change of heart and shows some humility, I'm willing to talk about the grounding again in the morning, with some revisions."

I realize that this cannot always be the solution. In regard to parenting, if you've grounded your kids for a solid two weeks, they need to see your consistency in order to respect you as an authority in their life. But today's situation was presenting an opportunity to teach my son a valuable lesson about God's nature.

I praise Jesus that sometimes He has given me a reprieve and shown me mercy when I didn't deserve it. I remember in the Book of Isaiah, King Hezekiah was on his deathbed as

Isaiah prophesied to him that he was going to die. However, Hezekiah turned his head to the wall and wept to the Lord. He asked for mercy. God's heart was moved and He gave Hezekiah another fifteen years of life. I want my sons to see God in that same light—the God who is moved when we sincerely come before Him with brokenness and humility. The way they are going to see that is through me, the person who is their earthly portrait of authority and parenthood.

I stayed in my bedroom for a few minutes and asked God to guide me through this conversation with my son. Then I called my sweet, teenaged, middle son to sit with me in the family room so that we could have a heart-to-heart talk. Since I had just prayed, I expected him to hear my words and receive them with joy and repentance. I envisioned him falling at my feet and crying out, "Mother, I've sinned! Please forgive me. I will obediently serve out my sentence today and I'll joyfully receive your gift of a new start tomorrow." However ...

My sweet, teenaged, middle child decided to refuse my offer and stormed off. He was angry that he would still have to see the grounding through today and would not be with his friends tonight. He was so stubborn that he couldn't even see the promise of having a great time tomorrow night with his friends if he would repent. As my son stomped off, I gently said, "This won't help you and may even make things worse."

My heart was broken, but not for my son. A realization hit me suddenly that my heart was broken for God. I had treated *Him* this exact same way.

I suddenly realized all the times that I've thrown a fit before God about something, then when He wanted to meet with me, calling me to prayer or Bible reading, I resisted and didn't want to humble myself to hear Him out. I only wanted the instant gratification I was craving to get things *my* way. Sometimes I chose to remain defiant and stay in my fit for days. In turn, I only made things worse and wasted valuable time with the One who loves me so much. In the process, I must have broken His loving, fatherly heart. Oh, I am so sorry for all those times that I turned Him away. What a fool I was. Yet, He was patient.

My son slammed the door to his room just to make sure that I had correctly interpreted his anger. As a nurturing mother, I wanted to go to him and make amends, but I heard the Lord speak in my heart. "Give him some time. Repentance needs to be worked in the heart. It is not just a short 'sorry' in exchange for a favor; it is something that the Holy Spirit wants to work in him. That work is continuous and fruitful."

That was about two hours ago. I have noticed that my son's words are becoming softer and losing their hardness and anger. Maybe by the end of the day they will be sweet and sorrowful, that's what I'm hoping for anyway. It's my true desire to restore the relationship and communion between us and for him to enjoy his day tomorrow. That is God's heart for us too. His desire is always to restore our communion with Him and for us to enjoy our lives. He's always willing to go meet in the family room for a heart-to-heart talk. Isn't He good?

Why write this chapter? Because there are some times when I still blow it. Although God has brought me a long way, there are still days when I am in the flesh and not in perfect tune with Him. Sometimes my anger at a situation overrides the moving Bible devotion I'd had just hours earlier or my frustration with people spills over into other areas in my life, causing discord. There will most likely be days when you will blow it too. But there is something that we can always count on: His mercy is great and it's available 24-7!

You need to believe in the mercy of God. You need to believe, that whatever comes your way, God's mercy is great, and His compassion is endless. That means if you aren't perfect in your dating life and make a mistake, God will forgive you. If you have been angry with God because you're not married yet, or because you've been through a devastating break-up or divorce, go to Him in prayer and talk to Him about it.

The point is not to wait for days before you appeal to God for that mercy. When you realize you have made a mistake, go directly to God and give Him a chance to show you how His mercy works. Don't prolong things and add further injury to yourself and others around you. Go talk to Jesus and you will find Him always happy to talk with you about anything.

I have a beautiful picture that I want to leave you with. My sister, Sydney, used to be a smoker (she's not anymore). My parents don't smoke and we were raised in a smokeless home, so naturally my mother was a little horrified at the sight. But Sydney had quite a habit and when we had family gatherings she excused herself every few hours to go sit outside alone on the back porch and smoke. My mother held her tongue but it was obvious that she had a disdain for the nasty habit.

My sister lives on the other side of the country so we only get to see her once a year for a few days at Christmas. One year my mother was so happy to see Sydney that she just wanted to spend as much time as she could with her. I passed through my kitchen one day and looked out the window to see my sister sitting on the porch smoking…and my precious mother sitting right beside her talking to her as if she didn't even notice the cigarette. My mother's desire to spend time with Sydney graced her to be able to look beyond the cigarette in my sister's hand and just be there.

I have reflected on that scene many times, as I have been able to see a picture of Jesus in my mother's actions. Jesus just wants to spend time with us and He will even sit down with us and our nasty habits and talk with us without harping on all the imperfections in our lives. That is mercy; a heart of charity and a disposition of compassion for people. Jesus is all about people and he is definitely all about you—imperfections and all.

So when you have blown it and you're having a bad day, exhibiting a little moodiness or just throwing a fit, sit down and have a talk with Jesus. Don't wait—just do it. God's mercy is greater than all your sin and He has seen it all, so just be real and talk to Him. He will be there.

CHAPTER TWENTY-FOUR

Can You and I Really Trust God?

Last year I found myself in a precarious situation. I was laid-off from my job. Oh, how it hurt! As a single mother, I had to resist the urge to sink into despair. I had to trust God—day by day, I had to trust Him. For seven long months, I had to trust. Seven months!

The first few weeks were hoped-filled. I knew I would have a job soon. I have always been able to gain employment, so I wasn't too worried. I submitted several resumes every week. In fact, the first few hours of every day were devoted to prayer and then job seeking. However, after a couple of months, reality set in and I was still unemployed. I realized it might be awhile.

After about four months, although I still had not landed a job, I realized that I was seeing some supernatural provision from the hand of God. My house payments were being made and I still had my car, food, gas money, and my friends and family. I hadn't lost anything ... except my pride and that was a good thing.

I *did* experience the questions from those wonderful, negative people in our lives who seem to love to challenge us in our hard times. "When are you going to get a job?" "Have you sent out any resumes?" (What a great idea! I wish I had thought of that ...) "Maybe you're just being too picky and you should just take anything." But I wouldn't let them get through my wall of faith. I was doing everything I could and God was providing and watching over me and that was my peace.

After about six months, my boys and I loved the fact that I was a stay-at-home mom. Life in our household was orderly and mom was home to cook, clean, and make my sons' lives as pleasant as possible. Not only that, since I had more time to pray over my sons, God had revealed some areas that needed immediate attention in their lives. I was able to focus on those areas and pray through them. I still was hoping, praying, and wondering about my new job - where would it be, what kind of people would I work with and when would it happen? But my hope never waned. I knew it would happen. I just kept applying for jobs and praying. Sometimes I cried while I prayed, but I did keep praying.

One of the few times I actually got an interview, I had a huge decision to make. The job could be mine, but I would never be able to go to church on Sundays. I know to some people this would not be a deal-breaker, but for me it was a huge issue. As a single mom of teenaged boys, I had always promised God that I would raise my kids in church. The truth of the matter was that I was the *only* person in their lives that would see to it that they were in church. It all fell on my shoulders. I knew that once my kids established a routine of missing church, my family would be in trouble.

Not only that, I was already facing some conflict with the kids about church. I wish I could believe that, left to their own devices, my teenage sons would get themselves up on Sunday mornings and be at church, on time, and in their places, but I know a little bit about teenagers. They're sneaky.

It was a crucial point in all of our lives. I felt that it was a test. I turned the job down and for the following week, I received a lot of grief from a few people. I'm sure that to some, it would seem like a very irresponsible decision. My heart was torn and I felt like I was all alone in my belief that God just had something better in mind. If it weren't for my best friend, who is the most faith-filled person I have ever met in my life, I would have crumbled under the pressure.

Something happened in my seventh month of unemployment; doors began to open. Finally, calls were coming in and I was being selected for interviews. Then it happened and I was blessed with a wonderful job at the highest salary I had ever made. They even gave me a higher salary than I had asked for. The job was perfect for me in every way—location, hours, people, and responsibilities. My boss was a wonderful Christian man and we loved talking about our churches. It was the best job I have ever had.

It was worth the wait! People called to congratulate me and I gushed to them about all the wonderful perks I was experiencing. God answered my prayers. It took awhile, but He answered with His best for me.

I wondered in my heart: if I could pray and seek God for the perfect job, why couldn't I trust Him to do the same for me regarding my future mate? In fact, short of our salvation, what is more important than choosing the person with whom you will become one flesh?

The months I spent waiting on God for the right job gave me insight into the nature of how things work sometimes in our lives. Maybe our hopes in waiting for a mate are the same kind of pattern as the one I found myself in while waiting for a job.

At first, we are full of hope. We think that it could happen any day. People around us are falling in love and we just know that our time is coming soon. But, after a while, reality sets in. We're still not married, and there are no prospects on the horizon. In fact, as far as the eye can see, there is not even a hint of anyone interesting out there. We start realizing that our only hope is going to be from God himself.

After awhile, we become relaxed in our single state. We realize that God's provision is real and we have all we need. Our friends and family are there for us and we haven't lost anything except our pride ... and that's a good thing. All the while, God is stretching our faith. Sometimes we think He's being too hard on us but then, we realize just how much stronger we really are. Our panic button doesn't seem to go off in stressful times. We're changing and the change has everlasting benefits.

At some time, a potential date appears and our hopes are stirred. However, we soon learn that dating that person might require some compromises in our life. Our morals and spiritual lives are not completely lined up with that person and we can see that he or she could potentially pull us down in our walk. Despite the encouragement of our friends and relatives, we decline and decide to pass up this great person for the one we know that God has set in our heart. No one understands this decision except our God and us.

Then one day the doors are opened. Calls are coming, new people have entered your life, and it finally happens. God has confirmed that this is the person He would like to introduce you to. As it turns out, this one is more than you had hoped for. This person is perfect for you in every way and you realize that he or she was worth the wait.

If God would do it for a job, would He not do the same for a mate?

Of course, He would! Don't let people distract you from trusting God. Forget the naysayers and the "faith-suckers" (people that can suck the faith right out of a room). What do *they* know about what God has in store for *you*? Sometimes we just have to learn how to silence the negative voices in our lives and remain strong in our faith and trust in God. I don't mean that you have to be rude to people and shut them out, but when they say something contrary to what you are believing God for, just politely smile and change the subject. You cannot reason with people who are without faith—don't even try. Faith is not within their realm of living and they won't understand it. However, when they see it lived out in your life, they may see a great example of how faith really works and a seed will be planted in their hearts.

God cares about every little detail in your life because He is a detail God. He knows best and He will bring it to pass when you and your future mate are ready. Don't let anyone steal your faith and don't let time be your enemy. Use this time to prepare yourself to be the best possible mate you can be. Stop saying that you are looking for a mate. Say that you are preparing yourself to be the best mate you can be.

You don't have to be perfect, just willing to let God work in you. Someday, it will happen, and then your friends will call to congratulate you and your life with that new person will be blessed. Stand firm and don't doubt.

Three Things That Will Change Your Life

I will instruct you (says the Lord) and

guide you along the best pathway for your life;

I will advise you and watch your progress.

PSALM 32:8, TLB

CHAPTER TWENTY-FIVE

When You Need Answers

Sometimes we need a breakthrough in an area of our lives in which we have prayed about for months or years and still haven't seen the answer. We have cried, sulked, and begged for something that we know can be ours, but for some reason, there seems to be a hold up. Sometimes we are really hungry for a blessing to be released in our lives; we just don't know how to move into that blessing.

Let me tell you what a friend of mine did.

Justeina was twenty-seven and a dear sister who was waiting on God for marriage. She was able to do this because of her strong personal walk with the Lord and her belief that He had a godly man waiting for her. She was also beautiful, fit, personable, and financially responsible. She was the total package. I just don't know how, in a church of 12,000 people, some lucky guy didn't fall for her and snatch her up, but it just didn't happen.

She yearned to be married. Ministry had been a big part of her life and she wanted to be a helpmate to someone in his ministry. Week after week, she devoted herself to activities and ministries at our church with her desire to marry tucked deep in her heart. She was a blessing to many people, including me. I never knew that she had such a desire to meet someone until she finally did meet him.

The news spread quickly that Justeina had been introduced to a man from another city, who was in ministry, and they were really hitting it off. When I caught up with Justeina, I inquired as to how this happened and here is what she told me. She fasted.

Turns out, a few weeks earlier, after an evening church service, she accompanied another girl out of the building and into the parking lot. As they walked along, they shared their desires to meet and marry. Both girls had been praying and seeking God but neither of them had met anyone yet. Although Justeina had fasted many times in the past, neither girl had ever fasted about this particular subject nor expressed a desire to seek God in this way. They agreed that they could encourage each other in this new spiritual venture and hold each other up in prayer. A pact was made and the fast was on.

Things began to move very fast for Justeina. Within just a few weeks there was a new man in her life. Within two months, she was engaged. Within another three months, she was married. She now lives in another state and enjoys ministry with her wonderful husband. By the way, and the other girl met her new husband too!

Now wait a minute ... before you run into your kitchen and start throwing out food so you can starve yourself until you meet someone, let's discuss a few things.

Fasting is not something you enter into lightly in an attempt to force God to do something on your behalf. It is a very powerful door through which we can seek and find God's will for our lives. It is also a spiritual force that brings things to fruition in our lives. There are simply some things that only come about as a direct result of prayer and fasting, and it may be hard, but very profitable.

I have fasted many times. Our church starts every New Year with a corporate, three-day fast, and I know many people who fast periodically throughout the rest of the year for continued guidance and major decisions in their lives. My church cell group just finished a fasting chain for one of the men in our group who was undergoing chemotherapy. Each day someone took a turn fasting and praying for this man's strength and healing.

My best friend and her husband are presently in a thirty-day fast for personal reasons. When I asked her why they entered this fast, she answered, "Because we are desperate for answers."

Every person who has been involved in fasting can attest to one thing: they do hear from God.

The first time I fasted regarding my dating life, it wasn't to find out when I would meet someone, it was to find out if God even wanted me to remarry. I wanted to submit fully to God's will as to whether I should remain single for the rest of my life or seek to remarry. It was hard to even entertain the thought that God might want me to remain single, but I felt that I had to present my whole life to Him as a living sacrifice and if that meant He had other plans for me, then I wanted to submit to the wisdom of His will.

Thank God, after fasting and prayer, he revealed to me *very* clearly that there is indeed a future for me with another person. When He revealed this to me, He followed up with confirming it through several other people. I also heeded God's leading to meet with my pastoral staff to submit to their wisdom for my life. I visited with the lead pastor of our counseling department and received a very loving and heartfelt blessing to remarry, another confirmation.

As you can see, I have taken several steps in seeking God's will for my future and most of these steps have been the result of time spent in fasting and prayer. The key outcome has been that I have heard from God, and when you hear from God on something, you can take it to the bank.

When you come to the point where you are absolutely sure that you want only God's best for your life, it's time to fast and discover His will. As God leads you into a fast, you can decide what kind of fasting you would like to do. Sometimes I have done a full fast from food for several days, and other times I have done a partial fast, such as a "Daniel fast" which involves eating mostly fruits and veggies. Usually my fasting involves abstaining from television and there have been many times that I have spent my lunch hour alone in my office praying instead of eating. Whatever is a sacrifice to you is what will please God. Just make sure that you are praying frequently throughout your fast and allowing God some uninterrupted time to answer.

When you are fasting, God will sometimes reveal many things to you in addition to the main purpose or goal of your fast. Or He may want to speak to you about something entirely different than what you had in mind. There have been times when God has taken my focus in a different direction than I initially started out. Instead of dealing directly with the re-marriage prospect, he revealed to me areas in my life that needed immediate attention and correction *before* I could begin to date. He does this because of our shortsightedness to all the areas of our life and His ability to see our "blind-spots." Preparation is very high on God's list of priorities for our future and a necessity for our success. There were also times when my fasting involved more of a relinquishing of my own will and desires than a direct answer to a question. As you continue to seek God you will most likely experience a transformation of your desires and new insights into who you really are, which will bring clarity as to the kind of person you should marry. This is all very important and will save you from making a wrong turn in your dating life.

When you fast and hear from God, your faith shoots through the roof and you can stand on that word through times of doubt. It's always God's will to give us a promise to hold on to when we are in a waiting period and when we fast He reveals many of those promises to us. It will be the thing that keeps you afloat until the time comes when you marry.

It's a good thing to read books to inform yourself about how to seek and find a relationship that will lead to marriage, but it all boils down to one important thing: what is *God's* will for your life? You must find out. Seek God and ask Him if He would have you fast to find out the next steps you should take. You may get some answers that give you a great peace, and you may even get a new spouse like Justeina did. You won't know until you do it.

CHAPTER TWENTY-SIX

If I Could Go Back and Do It All Again ...

As I look back through my life there is one thing that I wish I had understood when I was a small child. It is something that I believe would have changed the path of my life in so many ways and it is the most important thing I did after my divorce, changing me from the inside out. What I am referring to may come as a surprise to you: I'm talking about tithing.

I know that it is an uncomfortable word for some of you, but I would be doing you a terrible injustice if I did not write this chapter. Plus, I am not a preacher and I don't have a television ministry, so there is absolutely no motive for me to write this except to change your life. Please just hear me out on this—this is not a chapter about money—it's a chapter about Lordship and blessings.

Although I had been raised in church and heard many sermons on tithing, most of my experience had been just like the majority of Christians in America: when the offering plate comes around, you dig in your pocket for a few dollar bills and throw them in. And of course, I couldn't forget about the kids—before church on Sunday mornings, I rooted through my purse for spare change to give them to take to Sunday School. After everyone had given their "tip" to the Lord, we were all feeling pretty pleased with ourselves.

I was a very sporadic thither—when I had the money, I gave it. It wasn't until I became a member at my present church that I heard and completely understood the scriptural teaching on tithing. Boy, did it open up a whole new world for me!

After my divorce, when I began seeking the Lord again, I received a fairly large sum of money from my deceased father's estate. Since he had been a preacher who had given much money into the kingdom, he had carefully mentioned in his will that he would like the heirs of his estate to tithe 10 percent of their inheritance to the Lord. Although I was not a consistent tither, I respected my father's wishes and wrote out probably the largest tithe check I have ever written. It kind of hurt; but then, it kind of felt good, too.

Just two months later, God allowed me to buy my first home. It was a huge blessing to my children and me. We were so excited and it changed our lives. Our house was full of windows and sunshine and I called it my "happy house." My sons were thrilled, too, and since they helped me pick it out, they also took ownership in it. My boys, who had once been normal, teenage, sloppy boys suddenly turned into conscientious helpers around the house. They did dishes and laundry—*without ever being asked*. To this day, my sons still do their own laundry (and sometimes the dishes too).

That was the first of many changes that began in our lives. As I continued tithing on a weekly basis, God drew me nearer to Him and my heart began to change. My attitudes about money began to change too. As someone who used to be a binge shopper, I suddenly had no more interest in going to the mall. In fact, I started to hate shopping. All the old spending habits I had were changing and not only that, I was developing a real disinterest in credit cards. I stopped getting them and concentrated on paying off my balance.

Something was happening and I was becoming wiser in my financial decisions. I realized that God was doing more with the remaining 90 percent of my money than I had done with 100 percent. Money was stretching further, things stopped breaking down, and repairs on the car and house were virtually non-existent. I was being blessed at work, in my community, and in almost everything, I put my hand to. Things were happening in my spiritual life that had never happened. Somehow, tithing had opened doors for me in more than just financial avenues; it gave me a new understanding of the Kingdom of God.

Within three years of my divorce, I had more equity in my new house than I'd had in my other house during the sixteen years of marriage to my former husband. I was actually worth more as a single mom than when I was married and we lived with two incomes. It was a huge blessing to me because I did not receive any money in our divorce settlement. It became clear that God was my source. Not my ex-husband, not my job, my parents, or anything else. Only God.

Tithing as a single person is the most exciting and important thing you can do. It will take you to new heights as a giver and it will change you in many ways. It also puts you in a special covenant with God in which He will *always* provide for you. Being aligned with God in His perfect will is the most peaceful and reassuring existence you will ever know. It is absolutely wonderful!

Let's explore what tithing really is. I apologize that we cannot get into an in-depth scriptural study on tithing. I highly recommend that you read *When God Is First* by Mike Hayes. This book changed my whole view on tithing and putting God first in my life, and I have never been sorry that I made this a discipline. Here are just a few short things that tithing teaches us:

- It establishes God as the ultimate Lord of our lives. Our money represents our lives. It is the primary way that we are compensated for our time and our talents. We spend the majority of our years earning money for our families and ourselves. In giving God what is His—the tithe—we acknowledge that everything belongs to God, including our lives.

- It sets up a system of putting God first in every other area of our lives. As we honor God with our first fruits, we become more keenly aware of other areas in which we are not making God first.

- It is a spiritual law that was set in motion when God created the world. The more you give, the more you have. Even people who are not Christians profit from the spiritual law of giving.

- God can only bless what we give Him. This works in all areas of your life. When we hold onto things, it keeps God from being able to work in that area of our life. We have to learn to give God every part of our lives so that He can mold it and make it into what only He can. Moreover, when we give God His 10 percent, the remaining 90 percent is multiplied by God's blessings.

I could not write this without telling you that there have been some tests along the way with my giving. There have been times when I've been laid off from work and experienced setbacks like everyone else. God does not promise that we will never have any problems; He promises that He will carry us *through* all of those problems. I determined even more to keep tithing in the hard times. I wanted to show God (and the devil) that I was in this for keeps and that I could persevere. I wanted to make those sacrifices for God.

There is a deeper spiritual lesson here that I must address. When Israel rejected Jesus as the Messiah, it was because they were only looking for a Messiah who was a political leader that could save them from the Romans with a great military deliverance and set Israel up as the reigning kingdom on Earth. Since they were expecting a deliverance they could only see in the natural, they totally missed the *spiritual* deliverance that was happening right under their eyes.

Sometimes, we as Christians do the same thing. We are only looking for the deliverance we can see in the natural. We are looking for a check in the mail, or a lottery win to save us from our debts. We are expecting that our only salvation from our financial woes will be from some great downpour of funds through something such as a new job or wealthy relative. We are missing the point that as we are tithing, God is working a *spiritual* deliverance in us that is loosing us from our dependence on money and material things. From within, God is doing a great work and freeing us from the enslavement of the "money system" of the world. It is a wonderful and great work and if we are not careful, we can miss it and never know true freedom from the power of money.

This is one of the very powerful things that tithing does—it puts money in its proper perspective in our lives and changes us from the inside out. In a day and age in which the value of people is attached to their material and financial worth, this spiritual deliverance is pertinent in our lives, especially as we see the chaos happening on Wall Street with people losing their riches in stocks and trade systems. There has to be a deeper anchor.

I have always believed that when we pass a test, we are promoted. I've been through the fire I am still able to say that I have tithed through every bit of it. Consequently, I never lost anything in those hard times and my sons and I never went without. Not only that, I have seen God bless me financially in ways I had never seen before. I had never had someone walk up to me in church and slip a check into my hand before. And I had never had someone offer to take me to shopping for necessities for my family or fix something on my car for no charge—but I have now. I have had people offer things to me that have blessed me to tears and what *really* moved me was the fact that the very things they offered were things that only God knew I needed.

I was never a good receiver before, but I am now. I had always been a giver and receiving seemed shameful and needy to me. God spoke to my heart one day and told me that if I didn't learn to receive, I would be blocking a lot of blessings from *Him* out of my life. It turns out that the way God blesses us is through other people, the Body of Christ. If we cannot learn to receive from them, we cannot learn to receive from Him either.

Tithing has built, developed, and revealed character and strength in me that I never knew I had and has blessed me greatly. I'm hoping that it has blessed God too. Although I didn't start tithing until I was an adult, I sometimes wonder what would have happened if I had had the wisdom to start as I child. I don't wonder about the wealth I would have accumulated, although it wouldn't have hurt. But, I wonder what kind of spiritual wisdom I would have grown up in. Of all the things I wish I could go back and do spiritually, tithing is at the very top of the list. That is how much it has changed my life. I hope that my testimony will affect you. I leave you with these words from the Father:

"Test me in this [tithing]," *says the LORD Almighty, "and see if I will not throw open the floodgates of heaven and pour out so much blessing that you will not have room enough for it."* (Malachi 3:10, NIV)

CHAPTER TWENTY-SEVEN

Creating Your Legacy

Something terrible happened to me recently, and I must share it with you. My former parents-in-law, Richard and Judy, experienced a tragedy. They are the grandparents of my three sons, and they are still an active part of our lives, so the tragedy affected us all.

They were engaged in their usual morning routines when an accident occurred and there was an explosion in their house. Richard experienced the full impact of the explosion and was engulfed in flames, even breathing the fire into his lungs. He managed to make it out of the house and Judy also made it to safety, but Richard had been terribly injured. They called 911 and Richard, being the tough old man that he is, sat on the tailgate of his truck and waited for the ambulance. Within minutes he was on his way to the hospital.

I got the call after my ex-husband had arrived at the hospital. He was shaky and sober. "Dad's been burned in a fire, and the doctors are saying he won't make it. Get the kids and get to the hospital."

I tried to remain calm as I went to the kids' rooms and told them to get dressed. I gave them what little information I had and we headed to the hospital.

When we arrived, we were advised about what to expect when we saw Richard and then we were ushered into his room. Although he looked unrecognizable because of his burns, the same cheerful Richard spoke to us under heavy sedation. "Well, hello! It sure is nice of you all to come see me," was his greeting.

Although he looked terrible, he sure didn't seem close to death. However, the doctors gave us the grim prognosis that his death would be imminent within the next few hours. Because his lungs had taken in fire and over 80 percent of his body suffered burns, there was little they could do. They said his body would begin to swell, he would begin to dehydrate because his skin could no longer retain fluids, and then he would just drift off.

No one wanted to believe that in just a few short hours Richard would be gone. In fact, many people were angry. How could that be? He was still talking and very much alive.

It didn't take long for friends and family to start pouring into the waiting room. Anyone was welcome to come into Richard's ICU room and visit. The hospital staff wanted Richard to be comfortable with his loved ones around him.

As he drifted in and out of heavily sedated sleep, my energies were mostly focused on staying close to my sons and comforting them. It seemed so senselessly hopeless. I was praying in my heart. "God, what am I supposed to be praying here? Didn't you raise Lazarus from the dead? Am

I supposed to be praying for a peaceful, painless last few hours for Richard, or for a miracle?"

My oldest son had the same thoughts. "Why are they already talking about him in the past tense? Couldn't he still live?" he asked me. I could not answer him, I was confused myself. I wanted to believe for the impossible, but I was also wanted to understand God's will in this situation. Richard, although tough and hardy for his age, was sixty-nine. Recovering from severe burns like his would be excruciating and would no doubt be a battle for the rest of his years, but it was so hard to accept that it might be time to say goodbye.

Around 3:30 in the afternoon, I was talking to some relatives when my ex-husband appeared in front of me and said, "We need to go in the room, his blood pressure is dropping." I gathered my boys and we crowded in Richard's room. It was so quiet. No one really knew what to say. We formed a circle around the bed and held hands.

After a few minutes, his breathing stopped and we began praying. The medical instruments still indicated a faint heartbeat and we all watched the monitor in stony silence. Then, we saw the straight line and the machine sounded the signal as Richard died.

Everyone was still standing around his bed and my mind was racing. "If only I had known that this would happen, I could have made more attempts to see him and stay connected to him." I continued to mentally beat myself up. "Why does it seem that someone has to die for me to realize that I should have been kinder and closer to them?" I was half speaking to myself and half speaking to God. I continued, "But death happens so unexpectedly and how are we to know who we should be reaching out to?"

God then spoke in my heart. "Look around you—everyone in this room is going to die someday." I could say no more after that.

The more I thought about it over the next two days, the more I realized that maybe it was a good thing that the doctor spoke up and told the family that Richard wouldn't make it. His last day on Earth was filled with caring family and friends around him, loving him, and recollecting fond memories. Even the nurses commented on the number of people that were crowded into Richard's room. We were spilling out into the hallways so much that the hospital staff cleared the room next door to make an extra waiting room for all of us. More importantly, Richard had the opportunity to express his love for his family and even wrote out his final wishes on his pillowcase.

At his funeral, it seemed like our whole town was grieving. Richard had touched so many people in so many ways. It just goes to show what sixty-nine years of being kind to others can mean to those around us.

Now, when I think about my own mortality, I definitely want to be involved in the "group plan" (the Rapture). That has always been my hope—that I would be in the generation that gets to be taken out of this world before the Tribulation starts. But that still doesn't account for what happens in the meantime. Until that takes place, we are still mortal beings on a timetable. The Bible says that God has a designated number of days for every one of us.

But let's get our minds off our own mortality and onto that of those around us; they are on an allotted time, too.

Their days are numbered and God has not shared with us when their time will be. That means we must act as if it could be any day.

I don't ever want to attend another funeral and ask myself the question I asked two days ago, "Why didn't I …?"

When Jesus said, "Love others as yourself," doesn't that mean to treat them the same way you would treat yourself if it were your last day on Earth? I always hear people say, "Live as if it were your last day," but I never hear them say, "Treat people like it was *their* last day on Earth."

This is hard. How can we live this way toward everyone? What about those people who are constantly challenging us?

I believe that God gives some of us light on things that other people have not received yet. Everyone operates in the light that he or she has. Some of us have active prayer lives and read our Bibles so that God is able to shed a lot of light on the situations in our lives. Through our study and the guidance of the Holy Spirit, we learn how to conduct our daily lives in a way that produces good fruit. We learn to overcome evil with good, to turn the other cheek, and to do good to others, even when they may not deserve it. Some of the good fruit that is produced is remembered when we pass on. It is part of our legacy.

However, not everyone is in the Word every day and seeking God in prayer. Most likely, those are the ones that are argumentative, boastful, and just plain ugly sometimes. We need to understand that they are operating in the *only* light they know, which is somewhat dim and largely affected by the world around them. Somehow, it's just easier to have compassion and patience with people when you realize that they are operating in a shallow and limited understanding of Jesus' teachings. They have robbed their own lives and are victims of their own ignorance. It makes it easier to say under your breath, "Father, forgive them; they really don't know what they're doing."

I was reading in the Book of Acts this morning about Paul, a fellow single person. He was telling the Jews in Jerusalem about how at one time, he was a zealous persecutor of the Christians and even guarded the coats of those who stoned Stephen. That means that Paul observed the last dying moments of sweet, forgiving Stephen.

As Stephen was being stoned by the angry, ignorant people around him, he looked up to Heaven and prayed, "Father, forgive them, for they don't know what they're doing." He wasn't thinking about his own death, he was thinking about *theirs*. Thus, he's been immortalized as a saint around the world since that time because that's what the world longs to see—forgiving and loving people.

We need to reflect long and hard about the kind of life and legacy we want to leave. I have asked the Lord many times that if He delays His coming and I die before that time, I want my death to glorify Jesus. I hope that if I'm on my deathbed and people witness my last breath, they are able to say, "She loved Jesus with her whole heart and followed His commandment to love everyone." I hope there are happy memories and recollections of my kindness to others, and inspirational testimonies of how I was a witness for Christ. I hope stories surface about times that I sacrificed my own comfort for others. And most importantly, I hope my sons get to hear it all and can know without a doubt, that their mother is in Heaven checking out her new mansion with Jesus. That is the legacy I want to leave whether I am single or married.

You see, whether you are a single or a married person, you are creating your legacy right now. You are compiling memories for those that you will leave behind and you're laying up treasures in Heaven. Throughout this book, I have tried to encourage you and offer you hope in what your future holds. If it is your desire to marry, then I pray that God fulfills that desire with someone more wonderful than you have ever imagined or dreamed. However, I am also hoping that the paramount message of this book has a deeper meaning to you and that you gain much more than just a spouse. I believe that your willingness to let God be the Lord of your life will be the seed that brings many everlasting harvests to you.

When your time comes, your family and friends will have a legacy to remember you by. I hope that the legacy will be that you kept the faith, forgave a lot of people, spoke well of others, and kept hope alive for those around you. Most of all, I hope that you can meet Jesus and He will say to you, "Thank you for believing Me!"

Our life is a journey. Most likely, you won't always be single and you will marry someday. But while you are waiting for your perfect "someone," don't forget to let the love of Jesus shine on everyone in your path. If you can do this, you are well on your way to being a blessing to all—including your new spouse.

When our church decided to change our Sunday night service format to include cell groups, I wasn't sure how I would like this change. But it turned out that I soon grew to love the new format and every other Sunday night I excitedly look forward to these meetings in which twenty-two of us meet at my best friend's house for Lifegroup.

As the leader of the group, I selected a series of studies in which we are learning how to be more like Christ, and those studies focus mostly on the parables He taught. A few weeks ago, we watched a video about The Good Samaritan set in a present day scenario. Afterward, we discussed the video, read some Scripture, and I challenged our group to look for opportunities to be a Good Samaritan the following week.

The Bible challenges us to be not only hearers of the Word, but doers also. I like to incorporate this principle into my daily walk as often as I can, so the next day I began praying for my group. I prayed for each person that God would give him or her a Good Samaritan encounter so they could *live* the Word out in their lives and not just read about it. After I had spent about an hour in prayer for them, things were settling down in my heart and I heard a small voice say, "What about you? Don't *you* want to learn more about the Good Samaritan in your life?" I immediately responded, "Yes." I quickly assumed that God would soon orchestrate a divine appointment for me to get to minister to someone as a Good Samaritan. However, this was not what he had in mind.

Jesus then whispered in my heart, "How do you think I know so *well* how a Good Samaritan acts?" My heart suddenly overflowed with a new realization—when He told that parable, He wasn't only giving us instructions on how to live, He was talking about *himself. He is* the Good Samaritan, and *I'm* the person who was beaten and left for dead. I felt an urging to go to Luke, chapter 10 and read the story again, but this time with a few differences.

A woman was going down from Jerusalem to Jericho, her name was Stacy. Robbers attacked her. They stripped off her clothes and beat her. Then they went away, leaving Stacy almost dead. A priest happened to be going down that same road. When he saw Stacy, he passed by on the other side. A Levite also came by. When he saw her, he passed by on the other side too.

But a Samaritan came to the place where Stacy was. When he saw her, his heart went out to her. He went to her, poured olive oil and wine on her wounds, and bandaged them. Then he put Stacy on his own donkey. He took her to an inn and cared for her. The next day he gave two silver coins and to the owner of the inn. "Take care of her," he said. "When I return, I will pay you back for any extra expense you may have."

This is our Lord. This is our Jesus. He is the kindest, most caring person we could ever know and we get second chances in life because of *Him*.

At the beginning of this book, I told you how the world and the party crowd chewed me up and spit me out. I was hurt and broken after that. My condition went unnoticed by many and even good people passed me by, not because they were mean, just because they didn't know the sad state I was in.

One day my Good Samaritan, my Jesus, saw me and was moved by what He saw. When He saw me, He came to me and knelt down beside me. Then, He carefully inspected my wounds and began to pour soothing, anointed oil on them. He tenderly wrapped bandages around me and all the while He was saying softly to me, "You're gonna be okay, I'm here now."

In my weakened state, something in my heart began to inquire, "Abba, Daddy?" And He responded, "Yes, it's Me, and I will never leave you." He then, lifted me up and put me in a place where He could continue to nurse me and look after me. He does this through the comfort and guidance of the Holy Spirit, for Jesus is at the right hand of the Father preparing to come for us and take us home with Him. Some day He is coming back for me, and He has taken care to make sure that I will be provided for until that day comes.

I get teased sometimes for a particular saying of mine, "Jesus is so nice!" I know it sounds funny but I just can't help it. Sometimes when Jesus has done something kind for me, without a hesitation I gush those words out in their simplicity and honesty. Yes, maybe it is a gross understatement, but then maybe it's also a perfect way to describe Him. You see, it's the *kindness* of God that leads people to repentance, and when God was so kind to me after my divorce, I had no choice but to fall at His feet and ask, "Why are you so nice to me when I've been so bad?" His kindness is everywhere in my life and it makes no sense to me because I don't deserve it and I certainly didn't earn it.

He's kind because that's who He is. I see His kindness when I read about Him on the Cross taking the wrath of God on himself so that I wouldn't have to face it. I also see His kindness when on that Cross, going through His *own* agony, He was still ministering to others as He offered grace and peace to the thief hanging beside Him, saying to him, "Today you will be with me in Paradise.

I see His kindness in the story of Moses because I know that Moses is a picture of Jesus rescuing me from my enslavement to the world. He's my knight in shining armor, and the verse He gave me when He rescued me says it perfectly:

> *I am the LORD your God, who brought you out of Egypt so that you would no longer be slaves to the Egyptians; I broke the bars of your yoke and enabled you to walk with heads held high.* (Leviticus 26:13, NIV)

I especially see His kindness when I read the story of Joseph, knowing that Joseph is another picture of Jesus. I read how cruel Joseph's brothers were to him, selling him into slavery, and subjecting him to years of undeserved misery and rejection. (Jesus suffered that rejection too, from the whole world.) Many years later, when Joseph finally revealed himself to his brothers (because they did not recognize him), he forgave them and even fell crying upon their necks because he was so overjoyed to be reunited with them. They were terrified at that moment because he truly had the power to punish them. Instead, he consoled them, telling them not to be angry with themselves because it was all part of God's plan. Then I see the sweet kindness of Jesus, who is not angry with us in spite of the things we have done, and through tears He expresses to us that all is forgiven and that He yearns to have us in His arms.

I see another beautiful picture of Jesus' kindness and this one always moves me to tears. Someday Israel will recognize that Jesus is the Messiah, and just as Joseph forgave his brothers for rejecting him, Jesus will also forgive Israel. It will be a beautiful reunion of tears and happiness with Jesus consoling and comforting them. I can hardly wait for that day. What a beautiful sight it will be. See how nice He is?

My life of restoration began with Jesus and it will end with Jesus because He is the author and finisher of my faith. It is only appropriate that I leave you with a real glimpse of who He is, how kind He is, and how much He wants to put you and me back on the right track and give us a blessed life.

You will go through many stages and seasons in life as a single person, and most likely as a married person too. People will love you, and people will disappoint you. You will experience elation, and you will experience pain. You will have setbacks, and you will have victories. Some days your faith may be as high as the mountains but other days you may feel your faith waning.

However, just as the stars stay the same, one Person will always remain true and His never-ending love for you will be constant and unchanging. It's through His love that you will experience victories and great rewards and it's through His love and kindness that you will emerge from all the seasons of life stronger and more beautiful.

There is only one truth I have found that fits all the seasons of my life and it is the last thing I want to leave with you, for it has put all my failures and inabilities into perspective, and has surfaced as the highest triumph in my life. This one simple, truth has taken the focus off me and my inadequacies and has shone a brilliant light on the One whose love is matchless and wonderfully, incomprehensible.

That truth is: right now, this instant, Jesus is loving me and loving you. That love has never been stronger than it is at this moment and it will stay the same whether we are good or bad, deserving or undeserving, single or married. You are loved, accepted, and known, by Jesus and just as you love to say His name, He loves to say yours. He is saying your name right now ... over and over. He is breathing you in and exhaling His love for you. He is simply in love with you. Nothing can ever take this from you. Jesus loves you!